Life *after* Baby

Life *after* Baby

From Professional Woman to Beginner Parent

Wynn McClenahan Burkett

WILDCAT CANYON PRESS
A Division of Circulus Publishing Group, Inc.
Berkeley, California

Life after Baby: From Professional Woman to Beginner Parent

Publisher: Tamara Traeder
Editorial Director: Roy M. Carlisle
Managing Editor: Leyza Yardley
Production Coordinator: Larissa Berry
Copyeditor: Jean Blomquist
Proofreader: Shirley Coe
Cover Design: Eleanor Reagh and Jeff Wincapaw
Interior Design: ID Graphics
Typesetting: Terragraphics/Margaret Copeland

Typographic Specifications: Text in Berkeley Book 10.5/15, headings in Berkeley Bold Italic 12/15.

Printed in the United States of America

Library of Congress Cataloging-in-Publication Data
Burkett, Wynn McClenahan, 1959-
    Life after baby: from professional woman to beginner parent / Wynn McClenahan Burkett.
        p.cm.
    Includes bibliographical references.
    ISBN 1-885171-44-7 (pbk.: alk.paper)
    1. Mothers—Psychology. 2. Mothers—Attitudes. 3. Mother and infant.
4. Infants (Newborn)—Care. I. Title
HQ759 .B8 2000
155.6'463—dc21

                                                        00-036816

Distributed to the trade by Publishers Group West
10 9 8 7 6 5 4 3 2 1   99 00 01 02 03 04

To my family

Contents

Acknowledgments

A book like this is by nature a collective enterprise. I'm especially grateful to Tamara Traeder, Roy M. Carlisle, and the rest of the Wildcat Canyon team that took this project from "conception" to "birth." Without their dedication, sensitivity, and belief in the project, it never would have happened.

I gratefully acknowledge the many new mothers who shared their stories and insight with me about the transition to parenthood. I learned so much from these women — their candor and wisdom was what made working on this project such fun. In particular, I thank the founding members of the Golden Gate Mothers' Group who helped create a support system for me and literally hundreds of other new mothers in San Francisco. Special thanks to my dear friends and trusted advisors in parenting, especially my sister, Kristin Bradach, who is not only a great sister and mother, but a thoughtful editor.

Finally, I thank my husband, Bill, and my daughters, Elizabeth and Katherine, for their unwavering support and good humor throughout this long project. They rarely complained about the take-out meals or my anxiety level around deadlines. I dedicate this book to them with love.

A Word from a Parent

*My task was to redefine motherhood
in a way that made my children my
priority without losing sight of myself.*

This book came about because of the life changes I experienced when I became a mom. I am the insanely proud parent of the two most incredible children in the world. Before my first baby, I had spent the previous twelve years pursuing graduate studies and a career in business. As someone who viewed herself as a capable adult, I was confident that I was ready to take on motherhood. After all, I was a mature, competent woman — how hard could it be? I would add motherhood to my busy life without missing a beat.

Then, at thirty-four, I had a baby. To my surprise, being a mom wasn't quite like I thought it would be. I had never felt such heavenly joy and emotional disequilibrium all at the same time. Motherhood was a lot harder than I had anticipated. And not just because I had never changed a diaper before having a baby of my own. It was hard because I wasn't going to "just fit it in" to the rest of my life. This was a new endeavor that required *all* my attention. I wanted to be a good mother (whatever that means), yet I was going to have to learn how to be a parent without any training.

Before I had a baby, if I had a task to achieve or a problem to solve, I knew how to approach it. As a mother of a newborn, I didn't have any body of knowledge to draw upon. Plus my logical and intellectual skills didn't always do the trick. Having a baby was a lot more unpredictable than I had imagined. I was used to getting the job done and moving forward. With a small child, if I ended the day where I'd started, with a contented baby sleeping sweetly in her crib, I considered myself a success.

Here was the rub: I had worked long and hard to be taken seriously as a professional and had had no intention of having a baby and becoming a homemaker. But low and behold, here I was raising a child and managing a household. And although my husband and I had gone into it with an equal commitment to parenthood, I was struck by the disproportionate impact a new baby had on me as the mother. My task was to redefine motherhood in a way that made my children my priority without losing sight of myself. Like so many of us who had children after thirty, I knew that raising children was the most important job I could have. On the other hand, it was (and is) important for me to have activities that give me fulfillment outside the domestic realm. I still crave intellectual stimulation and a sense of accomplishment. In part, I satisfied these

2

needs by writing this book about and for new mothers.

My motto has always been "When in doubt, read a book," so when I became a new mother, that's what I did. I read everything I could get my hands on about babies, child rearing, and parenting. And yet I still didn't feel like my innermost concerns were being addressed. It wasn't until I started talking to other moms that I discovered that many women were experiencing the same sense of disorientation that I was. They had the same questions, anxieties, and guilt as I did. They too felt overwhelming love for their children yet resentful of the demands required in taking care of a small child. Phew. I wasn't a flop at motherhood. It was that after all those years of "being in control of our lives," we were embarking on something entirely unfamiliar.

It became imperative to me to develop a network of new mothers. I discovered that mothers of babies and toddlers live in a kind of social no-man's (no woman's?) land. We have to work at making friends and creating an infrastructure for support. Whereas parents of school-age children have the structure and community of school itself, mothers of new babies have to seek out their own sources of information and company. There are professional organizations for every other job, why not for moms? So I started a mothers' group in San Francisco. Now three hundred women strong, it provides new mothers a place to share information and support. I began to wonder, "Could new mothers get some of the same benefits of a mothers' group from a book?"

3

I decided to investigate this idea when my first child was just shy of her second birthday. I had started to get back some semblance of a life and my schedule was becoming more predictable. I knew I wanted to have another child but wasn't sure when. By the time I wrote the proposal, found a publisher and started interviewing mothers, I had had a second baby. Needless to say, that made writing a book more challenging.

People ask me why I would attempt such a thing. The answer is twofold. First I felt it needed to be done. I would have loved to have had the benefit of a book that presented real women talking in their own voices about what it was like to be an older mom. And second, what better time to do this than when I was in the middle of it myself? Sure, I'll probably have more perspective on the subject when my children are older, but I won't have that same burning desire to figure out how motherhood changes us in those early years.

The irony of trying to find time away from my children to write about being a mother is not lost on me. In fact, many would say that undertaking this project with two small children was utter folly. I don't completely disagree. Like all mothers, I questioned how much time I should be spending with my kids versus how much time I should be spending on my own creative endeavors. There were times when I didn't write for weeks because one of my children got sick, or the baby-sitter got sick, or the child with whom we had scheduled a play date got sick. It was on those occasions that I would say to my husband in frustration, "You know, if I didn't have kids, I'd be making a lot more progress on this book about motherhood!"

But I persevered because I wished I had had a book like this when I first became a mom. I will always be grateful to the "experts" who provided me with much needed information on child rearing, especially in those first several months. But I found that I was most comforted and reassured by other mothers. When sharing stories with other moms I felt relieved that I was not alone. I wasn't the only thirty-four-year-old woman who was daunted by introducing solids into my child's diet. I wasn't the only person with a graduate degree who secretly observed other mothers at the park to determine playground protocol. And I wasn't the only former manager who was outmaneuvered by a two-year-old at bedtime.

As I interviewed new mothers, I heard moving stories and heartfelt admissions. I hope this book will be a little like having a conversation with a group of trusted girlfriends — you know, the kind of special friends who weigh the merits of various diaper rash creams with the same intensity with which they discuss how to balance work and family. Although I have always thought of myself as someone who could figure things out by herself, I've realized that parenting cannot be done alone. Part of the reason I wrote this book is to acknowledge the collective nature of this journey into motherhood.

I leave the technical information and advice to the professionals. This book is about how it *feels* for an older woman to experience the transition to motherhood. As I was writing this, people would ask what my "findings" were. That was always a difficult question to answer because I hadn't set out to draw conclusions and wrap them up in a neat little package. Motherhood is messy in that way. We all experience things a little bit differently, and yet we have much to learn from each other. I wanted to share the thoughts and feelings of a collection of new mothers because that's what gives us a sense of proportion and makes us feel that we're not alone.

I have chosen to change the names of the women in this book although the stories, observations, and feelings are genuine. The women whom I interviewed were primarily over thirty, college educated, and had worked for several years before becoming mothers. Many continue to work. For the most part, they are married and in conventional relationships. They do not suffer from health problems, nor do their babies. Their situations are not extraordinary, yet they are doing the extraordinary work of being parents. I hope that the reader will benefit from the experience, insight, and wisdom they share within these pages.

O N E

Oh My Gosh,
I Have a Baby!

There's nothing like impending

parenthood to fill one with the

most magnificent plans.

And nothing quite like the

arrival of the actual baby

to puncture them.

— *Adair Lara*

*Making the decision to have a
child — it's momentous. It is to
decide forever to have your heart go
walking around outside of your body.*
— Elizabeth Stone

I consider myself a "planner," but no one could prepare me for what my life would be like after I had a baby. My tidy, predictable routine was turned upside down: there was no day and night, uninterrupted sleep was but a memory, and I (who once was known for never missing a deadline) couldn't get out of my pajamas by noon. And yet there were periods during my daughter's first few months of life that can only be described as blissful. I couldn't believe how much I loved this little baby. I couldn't believe how such a small person could be so demanding. I couldn't believe my own mother did this three times! How did an intelligent woman like me get myself into this situation?

One of the strangest things about being a new mother was that, at age thirty-four, I felt like I was starting over. After years of developing a sense of competency as a career woman, I found that my professional survival skills were suddenly irrelevant. I was a person who had gotten by in the world by using her brains, logic, and ability to communicate. As the mother of a newborn I had to rely on my body, my heart, and my intuition. And, believe me, they weren't always rising to the occasion. Talk about emotional jumble. One minute I'd be thinking, "This is fantastic. What took me so long to have a baby?" The next minute I'd be asking myself, "Now why was it I wanted to be a mother again?"

Do I Want to Be a Mom?

Some of my friends got married early and had children, and I wondered why they would want to do that.

For me and many of us who had babies after we turned thirty, becoming a mother was one of the many things we hoped to do in our lives. Whereas some in previous generations had children out of a sense of obligation or economic necessity, today's women don't feel pressured to produce an heir or provide another set of hands to work the farm. In fact growing up in the wake of the feminist movement, we also aspired to an education, financial independence, professional success, and personal growth. So why do 90 percent of American women have a child[1] at some point in their lives? We become mothers because we believe that the creation of a family will bring us joy, pleasure, and a deep sense of fulfillment.

Not all of us can pinpoint when we knew we wanted to have children. Although some, like Rosemary who had her first child at age thirty-one, always knew they wanted to be moms. Rosemary says, "I knew I wanted to have children ever since I was a little girl, and nothing in my life ever contradicted that. Part of it was that my cousins had a large family, and I loved spending time with them. If given the opportunity to pick what to do, my first, second, and third choices would have been to spend time with them. So for me, being with family was the most fun you could have. Of course, I also wanted to have a career, but I never really worried about how I was going to do both."

Many of us, though, emphasized developing our professional lives before becoming mothers. Carol, who was thirty-eight when she had her baby, says, "I wasn't against people having children, but growing up in the seventies, the track was to be self-exploring and to put your ideas and creative world first. I'm an artist, and every single female artist you read about has never been married successfully, let alone had a child. The models nurtured their careers, not other people. Some of my friends got married early and had children, and I wondered why they would want to do that. I viewed it as a betrayal of our social times. I know these women suffered because their peers didn't validate them. Now there's a big group of us getting hit by the biological clock and appreciating what they went through."

For most of us the decision to have children is made with a partner. In Janet's case, meeting the right man inspired her to get pregnant and helped her overcome her hesitations about starting a family. She says, "When did I first want to be a mother? I was never crazy about the idea, until I met my husband. He was a person who I believed would be a good father, a capable and equal partner in parenting. Before I had a baby, I was very aware that so much of the responsibility for raising children often ends up with the mother, and I didn't want that to happen automatically. Sharing the parenting responsibility is a big part of what's worked for us."

Of course, we don't always have the option to plan when we have a child. Laura describes how her first pregnancy at age thirty-two was a surprise and how she and her husband had to come to terms with having a baby before they had achieved their other personal and professional goals. She says, "Let's just say that when I announced to my husband that I was pregnant, it was not a Kodak moment. He didn't think we were financially ready to have a baby. He wanted everything to be perfect, and he hadn't reached the stage in his career where he felt we had achieved that. Also having a baby meant that some of our freedom would end. I think being pregnant for nine months is good because it gives you time to prepare."

I Can't Wait Any Longer to Have a Baby

Most of us know at an intuitive level when we're ready to take on motherhood.

The loudly ticking biological clock is a well-worn cliché. Yet for women over thirty, our age often *does* drive our decision to get pregnant and have a baby. With a good marriage, loyal friends, and an interesting job, we may not want to become parents quite yet, but there comes a time when we can't delay the decision any longer. Often our sense of urgency hits us suddenly and is triggered by an event that increases our sense of security (being promoted at work) or vulnerability (hitting a certain age).[2] We realize we don't want to miss out on becoming mothers because we waited too long.

Most of us know at an intuitive level when we're ready to take on motherhood. Pam says, "I don't know how to describe it. At age thirty, I just started getting motherly instincts." Or as Betsy related, "I had wanted to be a mother for as long as I can remember. I knew when I had children it would be the most important thing to ever happen to me. But when I was in college and during the years following graduation, I didn't think that much about it. Yet at a certain point in my late twenties, I remember a very real physical urge to become pregnant. We had our first baby when I was thirty-two."

Some experience the pressure to have children despite circumstances that aren't ideal for starting a family. Gina, the mother of a three-year-old son, says, "I always loved kids and wanted to have them. When I got out of college, I gravitated much more toward a career and had absolutely no interest in getting married because I wanted to work. I assumed that around thirty, I'd eventually settle down and have children. Being a mother was always part of the plan, but as I was getting older and not in a relationship, I got more depressed about it, desperate in fact. I thought, 'What do I do about this situation? Start dating?'"

Gina continues, "So when I was thirty-six, I tried to get pregnant even though I was single. It was a difficult, scary decision and I was very conflicted about it. I was unsuccessful, but I had been driven to the edge. I realized that becoming a mother was something I really wanted to do and this was how far I was willing to go to make it happen. In retrospect, I was relieved that I didn't get pregnant then. It would have been difficult emotionally for me. Fortunately, I met my husband not long after that and we have a wonderful son."

What If I Can't Get Pregnant?

Although the causes are not always clear, the simple fact is that as we get older, our fertility declines.

How ironic that we spend our lives trying *not* to get pregnant, then when we do decide we want to have a baby, we can't. In fact, close to 20 percent of the couples trying to get pregnant are currently experiencing infertility.[3] Although the causes are not always clear, the simple fact is that as we get older, our fertility declines. We've always taken our ability to have a baby for granted, and now we're in a situation about which we care so much yet over which we have so little control. Our feelings of powerlessness add to our disappointment and frustration.

We wonder if maybe we weren't meant to have children because it seems so hard for us compared to others. However, with time and medical intervention, many couples who had a difficult time getting pregnant eventually give birth to healthy babies.

Often those of us who experience more difficulty having a child enjoy more positive feelings about our pregnancy and birth. Jenny has a six-month-old and describes her situation this way: "I always had the expectation that I would be a mother someday. In my teens I logged in more baby-sitting hours than any of my friends, and really became close to a couple of children I took care of. In my mid- to late twenties I volunteered at a homeless shelter for mothers and children. I started wanting to have a child when I turned thirty-three. (I have no idea what was so special about that number.) It took us nearly three years to conceive and the longer it took, the sadder I got. I began to see myself as someone who would not be a mother. Two years of fertility treatments culminated in IVF [in vitro fertilization], and then we got lucky. My baby was born last summer and we're euphoric."

For some of us, not being able to have a baby of our own leads to a decision to adopt. Often we must give up our quest for the "ideal" family and examine our goals and priorities in a new light. We must come to terms with our feelings of failure, resentment, or grief over our inability to have a biological child before we can begin to embark on the time-consuming and emotional experience of adopting. And once the baby arrives, we may have mixed feelings about the placement. As adoptive mothers, we have many of the same logistical and psychological issues as birth mothers, without the nine-month gestation period to prepare. And yet the stories of satisfying adoptions are countless, and many of us ultimately come to believe that we were meant to be with our adopted child.

Going through the adoption process, however, can shake our confidence about our desire to be a mother. Deborah says, "I always knew that I wanted to be a mother. At age thirty-eight when I tried to get pregnant, it turned out that I couldn't. I was devastated. After years of fertility treatments I finally started looking into adoption, which I hadn't allowed myself to do while I was trying to get pregnant. It was interesting because as I was going through the adoption process, the clarity of purpose dissipated from me. I don't know if it was grief, or fear of the process, or intimidation. Maybe I was preparing myself that it wouldn't happen. But during the year that I pursued adoption, I never was clear, as clear as I'd been since I was a little girl, that becoming a mother was the right thing for me. Now that I have my son, I still feel like it's amazing that the two of us got each other. All the sadness and pain has evaporated because I feel that if anything in my life had gone differently, I wouldn't be with this child."

Having a Baby Is Scary

*The important thing about new-mother worries is to realize
that they are normal.*

What could be more exciting than becoming a mother–and
what could be more frightening! It's mind-boggling how many
new things there are to worry about as a parent. The act of
bringing another life into the world is awesome — the responsibility, enormous. And if that weren't enough, becoming a
mother is one of the few decisions in our lives that we can't
undo! Any rational person would be terrified. And yet we
need to remember that it's normal to feel anxious when we're
embarking on a new endeavor, and that we can have these
(not entirely unfounded) fears and still be good moms.

The wonder of becoming a mother is that you don't even
have to have a child for the fears to start surfacing. Most of us
begin to worry about our babies during our pregnancies.
Joanne has two boys and says, "My fears initially were during
the pregnancy itself, that somehow something would be terri-
bly wrong: a miscarriage, a birth defect. Every time I felt no
movement for a few hours, or even a break from the intense
nausea, I would call my obstetrician for reassurance."

Many of us have spent our adult lives in school or in a job
and haven't been around babies or new mothers. We wonder

what it's like to be a mom and to care for an infant. Megan writes about her concerns about motherhood: "I wasn't nervous about labor and delivery but was very anxious about being a mother. I think the entire enterprise was so overwhelming that I picked discrete absurd matters for worrying. For instance, I remember wondering how I would ever decide what the baby should wear. I would fold and refold all those darling tiny yellow and green outfits that you get when you don't know the sex of your new baby and wonder, 'How do you know when a baby is hot or cold or what a baby should have on?'"

Some of us have financial concerns. In the United States, the cost of raising a child over his or her lifetime is estimated at three hundred and fifty thousand dollars.[4] The mother of a newborn, Carla says, "I have financial worries. Part of it is not knowing what to expect, how much having a baby will really cost over time. I'm not sure what I'll be doing job-wise now that I have the baby, so I don't know how much money I'll be making. I'd like to take some time to raise my child myself and not have to work. There's a lot about our financial picture that we don't know, but we're hoping that by planning and saving we can manage."

We worry about how to integrate our new role as mothers into our lives as professional women. Many of us wonder how we will be able to continue in our careers and also be the kind of mothers we want to be. Kelly says, "One of my real fears was that I would lose my independence and sense of who I was. The transformation from a career-oriented person to being a mom was something that I was looking forward to but, at the same time, was very unsure of."

Then there is the fear that every new parent feels when we leave the safety of the maternity ward and are on our own with our brand new baby. Judy, the mother of a four-month-old, recalls, "I remember how scary it was to put the baby in the car seat to bring him home from the hospital. He was an average-sized baby, but seven pounds seemed so tiny. We were terrified knowing that we were going to be the first parents in the world whose child died on the way home from the hospital."

The important thing about new-mother worries is to realize that they are normal. We need to keep in mind that during our pregnancy and the postpartum months every aspect of our lives is shifting. It's natural to feel scared when so much change is going on. T. Berry Brazelton characterizes these anxieties as "normal signs of caring." He writes that our worries are "adaptive" and help us reorganize our lives for the big changes ahead.[5] Becoming a mother is a process of balancing those concerns that are real and need to be attended to, and those that we can dismiss because they don't serve any productive purpose in our lives as new parents.

Am I Bonding with My Baby?

Our initial feelings toward our new babies are as varied as we are.

The emotional bonding that takes place between mothers and their newborn babies is a real and important process. In fact studies have shown that in the first hour after birth, babies are alert, and that mothers and infants are particularly responsive to each other.[6] In light of this research, many hospitals have established practices and procedures in the maternity ward that facilitate this early attachment. And one of the advantages of choosing to do a home birth is that there is less interference in the bonding process.

However, just because bonding is desirable doesn't mean it always happens instantaneously. Although some of us expected bonding to occur the moment we laid eyes on our newborn, instead we felt detachment or relief. And in instances where there are health concerns for the mother or the baby, a physical separation may prevent an immediate opportunity for bonding. Despite the focus on the mother/child bond, one study showed that while 40 percent of new mothers felt an immediate bond with their baby, another 40 percent described their initial reaction as one of indifference. (Most of the mothers in the study, however, developed affection for their babies within the first week.[7])

Our initial feelings toward our new babies are as varied as we are. Whatever our reaction, it depends on our experience of labor and delivery, whether we had anesthesia or medication, how we feel about babies in general, our relationship with our husband, not to mention our basic health and personality.[8] The fact is that we may feel a variety of emotions at the birth of our baby: exhilaration, awe, relief, and sometimes even disappointment. Yet all these feelings are normal and acceptable.

Some of us felt a connection with our newborn because we started getting to know him or her during our pregnancy. Pam says, "I felt like a mother right away. When I was pregnant, my son was a really active baby. I felt like he was communicating with me even before he was born."

The affection and attachment we feel for our baby can be immediate. Joanne says, "When I first saw my son, I felt I knew him. His physical image was exactly what I had pictured. I felt enormous joy and relief. He was here and healthy. We had made it through together." Jenny and her husband underwent IVF in order to conceive and give birth to their child. She says, "I can't really describe how I felt when my daughter was born. Euphoric times infinity is a start. My mother would agree. She said that when I phoned her at 4:00 A.M. to give her the news, I sounded like I was calling from Filene's basement and it was the Chanel sale and I was the only shopper there."

Others of us were surprised that we didn't fall in love with our baby right away. Before we could focus on our babies, we needed a recovery period of our own. Many of us who had difficult labors were relieved the baby was healthy but were too exhausted and overwhelmed by the birth itself to feel connected with this new person. Studies show that the more difficult the mother's labor the less likely she is to form an immediate attachment to her baby at delivery.[9] Grace's experience is not unusual. She says, "I gave birth without any anesthesia. I was so wiped out when it was over that I just wanted to rest. I was happy that everything was all right, but I needed to regroup before I could bond with anybody. Of course, when they brought my daughter to me after I'd slept for a few hours, I was so enthralled I couldn't take my eyes off her. Yet I still didn't feel like she was really mine."

As Wendy remembers, "I had a C-section. I was pushing for two and a half hours. The baby wasn't coming out and her heart rate was getting low. I was exhausted and scared. I just wanted to get that baby out! They wheeled me into the operating room and when she came out, they whisked her away because of her low heart rate. They didn't give her to me. They wanted to make sure that she was okay, which she was, but it took five minutes to determine that. So more than bonding, I felt relief: this is over, she's healthy. They put her in my arms, and I have it on video. I said, 'What do I do with her now?'"

Many of us feel a strong physical bond to our baby right away, but we don't develop an emotional attachment until the baby is a bit older. The mother of a three-month-old, Heather felt an instant connection with her daughter but says that the tie was tenuous in the first weeks of her baby's life. She says, "Right after the baby was born, the midwife had to remind me to open my eyes and look at the baby so she could hand her to me. After the intensity of the labor and birth, she had to bring me back to the delivery room. As soon as I held the baby, I felt a connection that lasted the whole time I was in the hospital. Once we were home, there were times in those early weeks where I felt like whatever bond was there was very fragile. There were times when I thought that having a baby was just a pain, and that made me feel guilty and badly about myself as a mother. But our love evolved."

Going through labor and birth is a redefining event for most of us. It takes intense focus and concentration to deliver a baby. How we feel when this is over and how we feel upon meeting our new baby depends on a variety of factors and cannot be predicted. As pediatrician T. Berry Brazelton observed, whether we feel love at first sight or our love emerges in a more gradual way, all of us can go on to develop a healthy and lasting bond with our child.[10]

I Love Being a Mom, So Why Am I Crying All the Time?

The "baby blues" are attributed largely to the changes in hormonal levels that our body undergoes in the days after birth and as we start producing milk.

Being a new mother is about having every aspect of your life in a state of flux. Could we have any more emotions (often contradictory and unexpected) all at the same time? We go

22

from elated to desperate in a matter of moments — several times a day. And many of us were particularly moody around the time that our milk came in. Referred to in the literature as the "third-day blues," this state can occur anytime during the first two weeks after delivery and affects up to 90 percent of us.[11] The "baby blues" are attributed largely to the changes in hormonal levels that our body undergoes in the days after birth and as we start producing milk. As if sleep deprivation weren't enough, these hormonal changes can cause us to be *extra* sensitive and tearful. (Not just a result of physical changes, adoptive mothers may also experience the blues as we adjust to having an "instant" family.)

The blues can hit when we find ourselves all alone with our newborn. Tina's son is eight weeks old. She recalls how happy she was when her family came to be with her during the delivery, and how she fell apart when they left. She says, "The birth seemed like such a celebration to me. I was on a high. The baby was born on a Thursday, and slowly people left one day after another. Then on Monday, my mom left and my husband had to go back to work and that's when I lost it. I just cried. I cried if you did something nice. I cried if you didn't do something nice. I just sobbed for twelve hours straight. And even if I was happy, I was crying. I hit that wall."

As many of us know first-hand, uncontrollable mood swings can accompany our milk coming in. A mother of two, Kathleen says, "When my milk came in I experienced a hormonal tidal wave. My main memory from that day is standing in our living room crying with my milk dripping as I told my husband I didn't think I was up to the task of keeping a baby alive. (It was a noble idea, but we really should just call the whole thing off.) Who would have guessed that several hours later I'd find myself contently sitting and gazing at my baby crooning 'I'm in Heaven!' to her pink, round face."

No One Told Me about Leaking

Despite its wonders, nobody tells you about the inconveniences of breast feeding.

So much of our first experiences of motherhood revolve around just keeping our baby alive. Our primary mission is to make sure that our newborn is thriving, and we are held captive by the new arrival's eating schedule. Given the proven physical and emotional benefits of breast-feeding, many of us intend to nurse our babies. In fact, among women with a college degree or higher, over 80 percent of us nurse.[12] For many of us, breast feeding is a uniquely sweet experience. It's the one thing that we can do for our baby that no one else can do. And once we've gotten nursing under control, there's nothing like giving our baby mother's milk to make us feel powerful and maternal.

LeeAnn describes how much pleasure she got from nursing her daughter: "I enjoyed it so much. I thought it was one of the greatest experiences. It was such a feeling of nurturing. It was a continuation of the whole process of giving birth: giving life and seeing your baby grow, knowing that you were so directly helping her to become a healthy baby. I experienced a real feeling of fulfillment and deep connection. I have such wonderful memories and feelings of an incredible closeness. I felt so needed, and I was satisfying a need that was so essential. And the closeness was so exclusive between the two of us. When I stopped nursing I felt a little like I had lost my special status and was just like everyone else now."

Despite its wonders, nobody tells you about the inconveniences of breast-feeding. Heather, who has a three-month-old, says she was unprepared for the mess. She relates, "I'm really glad I'm nursing my baby. I love breast-feeding, but nobody told me about leaking. I guess I'm a good producer because I leak constantly. I've stained all sorts of good shirts. I didn't anticipate the indignity of it all!" Yet she continues by describing the intimacy of nursing: "Unfortunately, my daughter still gets up two or three times a night to eat. I try to savor the private time we have in the dark of night. I love how she cuddles with me after feeding as she falls back to sleep. I know this won't last forever so I'm trying to enjoy every moment that I can."

Although we may dream of sitting in a handcrafted rocking chair with a baby peacefully at our breast, feeding a newborn doesn't always come easily. It takes persistence and dedication. In many cases, both the new mother and the new baby must be taught how to nurse. And although in many parts of the country the resources for assisting new mothers are plentiful, getting started can be frustrating and painful.

Our feelings of inadequacy may be compounded by the fact that nursing is something we feel we *ought* to be doing easily and naturally. Betsy describes her efforts to get her baby to eat. She says, "Our baby was two weeks early and all he wanted to do was sleep. He wouldn't wake up. (Meanwhile as each day went by, my breasts became fuller and fuller to the point that I was in severe pain. All of the glands under my arms were full of milk so I couldn't put my arms by my sides.) When he did wake up he was unable to latch on so he would scream inconsolably for long periods of time." She continues, "After about five days, when I was at the end of my rope, someone suggested a breast pump. My husband found a medical supply shop and came home with an electric breast pump that finally solved the problem. Throughout all this, I was determined to make breast-feeding work. It seemed to me to be one of Mother Nature's most basic and important arrangements, and I was not going to 'fail' at it."

Mothers of twins have special challenges when faced with keeping two hungry babies satisfied. Heidi is thirty-six and her twins are five months old. She describes how constant those early feedings seemed: "At first, I was nursing both babies at the same time. It was very cowlike. I felt like I'd been reduced to an animal. At three weeks, I nursed them individually. They were supplemented with formula from the begin-

26

ning, but it felt like I was constantly nursing. In between, I was trying to sleep or eat so when I was done doing those things, I had to feed them all over again."

Others of us try breast-feeding but stop when faced with our discomfort and concern that the baby is not getting enough nourishment. Laura recalls, "I was not a big breast-feeder. It was physically painful and messy. I didn't produce enough milk because I was so exhausted and didn't have any help. I wasn't eating enough and my milk started drying up, so we went to the bottle. I tried to nurse because I thought it was the right thing to do, but it turned out not to be right for us."

Some of us make the decision before the baby is born to bottle-feed. Amy, who had her daughter at age thirty-eight, works in the health field. She says, "I had no interest in breast-feeding. I knew from the get-go that I wasn't going to breast-feed, and it was a fabulous decision for me. I'm someone who does not function at all without sleep. I knew I had to be back at work in eight weeks, and I had to be able to do my job. With bottle-feeding, other people could help me. It's worked well; my daughter is healthy and happy."

Although the benefits to the infant of breast-feeding are indisputable, the decision to nurse or bottle-feed is ultimately up to each of us. We need to be confident in our choices and surround ourselves with people who support the decisions we've made. More often than not, breast-feeding doesn't come easily, and both mother and baby need to be educated to make it go smoothly. It's important to get the help we need —

whether it's from a nurse at the hospital, a lactation consultant, or another mother — and to not feel like we're "bad moms" if breast-feeding is difficult or we decide it just isn't for us.

I'm Bewildered by My Emotions

However it's defined, the postpartum period is characterized by fatigue, feedings, and frayed nerves.

In the medical world, the postpartum period officially lasts six to eight weeks. During this time we are healing from the delivery and our uterus is returning to its prepregnancy size.[13] (With respect to work, the postpartum period is considered three months. Since 1993, the *Family and Medical Leave Act* requires employers to provide up to three months [unpaid] leave after the birth [or adoption] of a baby.)

However it's defined, the postpartum period is characterized by fatigue, feedings, and frayed nerves. We are torn by the unbearable love we feel for our baby and the unglamorous tasks we must perform in caring for him or her. Julia says, "I remember a friend calling me up and saying the first few months are boot camp. You have to get geared up for it. When you're in it, you don't even realize how hard it is until you're out of it." Kathleen describes it this way: "No one can prepare you for what awaits for you after the birth of your first child. My life was topsy-turvy. The concept of symbiosis was brought home to me in new ways as I realized that my baby and I could not get our respective needs met at the same time; my shower would just have to wait until tomorrow. The really unbelievable part was how totally ecstatic I felt in the midst of all the chaos. I remember telling an expecting friend on the phone that the baby had totally ruined our life and we were so happy."

Many of us are not completely confident in our mothering skills and are fearful that we'll do something traumatic, if not outright harmful, to the baby. Lucy, the mother of a thirteen-month-old son, recalls, "The big event at age 3–4 weeks was changing the baby's diaper, especially during the night. My husband and I would wake up and say, 'Oh my gosh, he needs to be changed.' And we'd both get up to do it. 'You do the top and I'll do the bottom.' The person at the top would console him, while the person at the bottom quickly tried to change the diaper. We had no confidence in what we were doing."

Babies have been shown to become more sensitive to external stimuli and to cry more at age 3–4 weeks.[14] Unfortunately this seems to occur when the visiting helpers have gone home and the lack of sleep is starting to take its toll. The mother of a one-year-old, Megan remembers, "The first few weeks were blissful. Our son slept a lot; he looked darling; everyone loved him; my husband spent a week at home; my friends brought food; our relatives came from far and near for baby viewings. The house was clean; the gifts were put away; we knew the UPS man by heart. The birth announcements arrived and I started to address them. Then my husband returned to work and started traveling for work and the baby woke up. Suddenly my son was always awake and always crying. Suddenly I was always tired and the house was always on the verge of looking awful. I felt like my life was out of control. I got great advice from a friend who had a child about a year older than mine. She reassured me, 'He's your child and you love him to death but he's screaming for hours and it just totally sucks, and I don't mean a little.' I felt so reassured that it was okay to feel rotten about parenthood and so relieved that other parents felt the same way."

As the first several weeks go by and some of the initial euphoria wanes, it dawns on us that a mother's responsibilities are not only enormous but also unending. Especially as older mothers, it can be difficult to reconcile our individual needs with the insatiable demands of an infant. Jocelyn, a thirty-six-year-old graphic designer worked independently before becoming a mother. She recalls, "I had to get out of the house just to be by myself. I think part of it is that I'm so used to being by myself that all of a sudden to have someone attached to me was a big shock. That was the most amazing thing. I married later in life and was such an independent person, even in my marriage. My husband and I both traveled a lot and did things separately. Someone said to me that when you have a child, you just need to get a lot of help, but that's missing the point. It doesn't matter how much help you have because you now have this responsibility that's never going to go away."

Like an estimated 25 percent of first-time mothers,[15] Virginia suffered from postpartum depression. She says she was surprised by her emotions because no one talked about these negative feelings before her baby was born. She says, "I was fine when I was with the baby, but it was all the other issues I couldn't handle. I was used to dealing with a lot at the same time, and I just couldn't do it anymore. I remember being out doing an errand one day and thinking, 'I don't want to go home. I just want to run away.' Of course, I did want to go home, but I also wanted to escape. I didn't know about postpartum depression so I was really worried about how I felt. Once I was diagnosed, I refused to go on medication because I wanted to nurse. With the help of my husband and a therapist who worked with sufferers of postpartum depression, I finally got through it, but it was rough."

Somewhere between weeks 6 and 8, just when we think we'll snap, the baby begins to respond to us. As the baby smiles, makes eye contact, and follows us with his or her gaze, we fall head over heels in love and start feeling more confident in our mothering skills.[16] Betsy describes this transition from frazzled caretaker to adoring mom. She says, "My baby would screech for long periods for no reason I could understand or figure out. He would cry, that high-pitched newborn wail, for anywhere from five minutes to two hours any time of day or night. I would pace the floor with him in the middle of the night with both of us crying, feeling as if I had made the biggest mistake of my life. Why had I thought I wanted a baby? Where had all these images of peace and bliss come from? I wanted my old life back. I wanted some control over my life again. Overnight I was no longer in control of anything. This little, scrawny, screaming miserable baby controlled every aspect of my life."

Fortunately for us, babies change dramatically in a short amount of time. Betsy continues, "I was so eager to go back to work those first six weeks. I called the office, I dreamed of work, I thought about it constantly. I couldn't leave the house for fear my baby would start screaming and I wouldn't know what to do. Where were those natural instincts I was supposed to have? Then, at six weeks, my baby smiled at me and my heart melted. At three months he settled down and was an entirely different child. He was the most beautiful baby I had ever laid eyes on, and we were madly in love with each other."

My Baby Won't Stop Crying

Colic often affects how we feel about motherhood.

All new parents live in fear of the dreaded colic. Although an estimated one in five babies suffer from it, no one is sure what causes colic, which makes it impossible to "treat."[17] For the mother of a colicky baby, all the "normal" ups and downs of the postpartum period are exaggerated. And no one can be prepared for the stress that accompanies the overwhelming task of caring for an infant that is inconsolable. Carol, whose son is eight months old now, describes life with a colicky baby this way: "I knew nothing about babies. We had a baby nurse come and from the minute she met my son she knew that he was really high-strung. She looked at me and she said, 'You're going to have a tough time.' She knew. He cried six to eight hours a day. Walking him didn't seem to help. I couldn't even take him outside because he cried all the time. People would look at me like I was a child abuser. My son can still cry longer and harder than most babies."

As much as we'd like to, colic is not something we can control or "fix." Carol goes on, "It was the hardest time I'd ever had in my life. I'm a type A kind of person. I get things done. I put my nose to the grindstone. I figure it out. But in this situation that strategy was wrong, wrong, wrong. There is a kind of dementia about that period. I've edited out a lot of those days, because I just don't want to think about it. But I was very comforted by my friends. They knew I was having a hard time and they were very honest about how hard it had been for them with their new babies."

Colic often affects how we feel about motherhood. Antonia describes how her first child suffered from colic: "My baby was really colicky, so my first experiences with motherhood were awful. The first three months of his life were miserable. It was not that picture of bliss I had imagined: wearing a fluffy white nightgown and gazing into my baby's eyes. I had a horrible pediatrician who said, 'You need to love your baby more.' Even as new parents, we knew enough to change pediatricians. The second doctor told us to make sure we took care of ourselves, which was much better advice."

I Didn't Know I'd Feel So Isolated

We love being a mother, but how do we describe what we did all day to a colleague who doesn't have children?

At times, all first-time mothers feel isolated during the postpartum period. This loneliness may be particularly hard for older mothers because we thought we had a well-developed social network. But think about it: many of us live apart from our extended families and friends. We rarely know our neighbors. Most fathers go back to work shortly after the baby's birth. And the built-in social life we had at work doesn't help when we're responding to the round-the-clock requirements of an infant. We love being a mother, but how do we describe what we did all day to a colleague who doesn't have children?

Feelings of loneliness can come as a real surprise. Heather, the mother of a three-month-old says, "I've always had so many good friends, but it's not like they're all around. I had no idea I'd feel so isolated with a new baby." Or as Grace reports, "I underestimated the importance of the social part of my job. When I was home with my daughter those first few months, I really missed being around other people. So much of what I was doing as a new mother required me to be at home by myself: feeding the baby, doing the laundry, and letting the baby nap. I didn't get out very much. I craved adult company. I'd pounce on my husband when he got home from work, because I was so eager to have someone to talk to."

Not having family around can also add to our sense of isolation. As the mother of a new baby, Amy missed her family and wished they could be around more. She says, "I have this huge family of sisters and brothers, and none of them live nearby. That was really hard. How will your baby get to know your family and your values if you don't spend time with each other? And it was hard for me that my mother is not alive, because my baby looked so much like my mother. It was incredible. Having a baby really makes me miss not having my family closer."

I Need Help

Since most of us don't have a tribe of aunts and older women who gather to help us through the transition, we must assemble our own community of caregivers and helpers.

Although many of us have spent years figuring out how to do things on our own, we quickly discover that when it comes to babies we need help. After being discharged from the hospital twenty-four to forty-eight hours after going through labor and delivery, we're expected to take on the role of mothers with little support or guidance. Since most of us don't have a tribe of aunts and older women who gather to help us through the transition, we must assemble our own community of caregivers and helpers. Often our parents (particularly mothers) are the ones who come to help us during those first important days and weeks. Others of us may hire a professional caregiver such as a baby nurse, who is skilled at caring for newborns, or a "douhla," who nurtures and comforts the new mother so she can focus on her baby.[18]

In the first few days of our baby's life, our husbands are our greatest source of help and comfort. Many new mothers describe how wonderful it was to spend that initial period alone with their new family. Carrie's baby is five months old. She says, "One of the things that appealed to me about doing a home birth was that it allowed time for just cloistering in our own home. I felt like a completely different person after my baby was born, so it was very important for me to have that quiet space where I didn't feel pressure to lead my old life. My husband was great. He worked from home as much as he could so he could help me with the baby. It was wonderful — just the three of us in our little protected cocoon."

Many of us feel that after going though the intense physical and emotional experience of giving birth, we want to be with our own mothers. Jocelyn recalls her first few weeks as a mom. She says, "My husband took a week off and my mother came out for three weeks after that, because I knew I would need the help. I wasn't under any illusions that I could do it on my own. My mother was amazing because she took care of me. She cooked and cleaned and let me get out of the house so I could collect my thoughts. Her help was invaluable."

If family members are not available to help, we may turn to professionals who can nurture us. Joyce describes how helpful it was to be with women who were wise in the ways of babies and new mothers: "We had a baby nurse for three weeks and a douhla for three weeks after my daughter was born. They were instrumental in helping me become comfortable with the baby and with breast-feeding. They were both very nurturing. So I had a wonderful, full experience the first six weeks, because both these women were focused on helping me with the transition to motherhood."

Whoever provides it for us, support is crucial. As Marcia, a single mother, describes, "I was really overwhelmed with the support I got when I had my daughter. I had a great support group. I have a lot of close women friends who were really thrilled for me and came to my assistance. And my parents — it wasn't easy for them at the beginning, but they rallied. They helped enormously, and they adore the baby."

Thank Goodness for Other New Moms

Who but another mother can appreciate the fact that you got out of the house before lunchtime with your hair combed, teeth brushed, and shirt right side out?

The company of other new mothers cannot be overestimated in helping us to weather the ups and downs of the postpartum period. Their companionship helps us feel less isolated and provides us some much-needed perspective. We relish their compassion and humor, and look to these other women to validate our feelings and to understand what we are going through. Who but another mother can appreciate the fact that you got out of the house before lunchtime with your hair combed, teeth brushed, and shirt right side out?

Some of us are lucky enough to find support through organized groups for new mothers. Elise recalls how much comfort she got from a support group that met once a week at a hospital: "About three weeks after my daughter was born, I went to a mothers' group at the hospital. It was a fabulous starting point because it opened up a new social life for me. I had something in common with all these women I'd never laid eyes on before. That really started me on my way. And I was so excited because I had gotten out of the house on my own. I was so nervous to take my new baby out of the stroller and put her in the carrier, but I found this sense of relaxation being there with all these other new mothers."

It can also be important for brand-new mothers to find a friend with a baby very close in age. Now the mother of three, Samantha advises, "You need to find someone who is as interested as you are in new babies. You deserve to have somebody who wants to talk endlessly about labor and nursing and the first smile. It's not that a mother of three doesn't care or isn't interested, it's that she's distracted by other things. You deserve total fascination, concentration, and focus. And don't feel guilty or weird about it because it's wonderful and you should enjoy it."

In an ideal world mothers-to-be would anticipate their needs and begin putting their support system in place before the baby is born. But many of us are leading busy pre-baby lives and aren't focused on what it takes to be a new parent. The reality is that we're thrown into a new job and expected to figure it out on our own. No wonder we feel unprepared. During those first several months, it's important to get help and to acknowledge the range of thoughts and feelings we're having about the transition. And although it may be hard to imagine when we're in the middle of it, we need to remember that the postpartum phase is relatively short-lived. Most babies start to sleep more regularly and develop a routine around 10–12 weeks. And often it's other moms — through a visit from an old friend, a chat on the phone, or a meeting of a new mothers' group — that help us appreciate the once-in-a-lifetime experience of having our first baby.

T W O

I'm Not Sure How to Be a Mom

Motherhood is the second oldest profession in the world. It's the biggest on-the-job training program in existence today.

— Erma Bombeck

*The commonest fallacy among
women is that simply having children
makes one a mother — which is as
absurd as believing that having a
piano makes one a musician.*
— Sydney J. Harris

Just because you gave birth to a baby doesn't mean you automatically *feel* like a mom. Becoming a mother is a process requiring us to integrate our new identity and priorities into our old lives. And while we're incorporating our new role as a parent, there may be periods in those initial months when we're not sure *who* we are anymore. Am I a mother? Am I a woman? Am I a professional? Am I a wife? We find ourselves thinking, "A few months ago I was a fully functioning adult. Today I'm an inexperienced caretaker praying that I can keep a baby alive! Where did the old 'me' go?"

Although some of us felt like mothers the instant we gave birth, most of us take longer to get into the part. Feeling like a parent may be precipitated by a specific event, such as the first time we nursed a sick baby, heard ourselves referred to as somebody's "mom," or blurted out a phrase our own mother used that we vowed never to repeat. But for most of us, becoming a mother is a complex process that influences our adult development and unfolds only with time and experience.

I Thought I Was Going to Be the Perfect Mother

*The images of motherhood we grew up with often conflict with
the day-to-day job of being a mom.*

Before having a baby, many of us had an idealized picture of
what we would be like as moms. Often we're not aware that we
even had this mental image until we become a mother and discover that our fantasy doesn't match the reality of caring for a
newborn twenty-four hours a day. In other cultures and social
times, how a child "turned out" was a matter of fate, genetic
predetermination, or an act of God. In contrast, we live in an
era where responsibility for a child's happiness and future success is placed primarily on that child's mom. This puts us
under subtle yet constant pressure to be "good mothers."

And although we have individual ideas about what constitutes a good mother, there are some iconic images that
influence us. In our culture, the "perfect" mother is loving,
understanding, and self-sacrificing. She is calm and cheerful.
The mythological mother never has a bad day. We soon realize that motherhood isn't quite like we thought it would be.
In short, we are much more frazzled than June Cleaver ever
appeared to be.

Universally our expectations about parenthood change
after having a baby. Megan describes her trip home from the
hospital as a new mother. She says, "After my baby was born

and as we were getting ready to leave, I took off the hospital gown and put on the outfit I'd so carefully packed about a month earlier. 'Memo to Self:' I thought. 'For future childbirths, do not plan to wear panty hose home from the hospital.' I think that was a sign of things to come — I had deluded myself into thinking that mothering could be accomplished in panty hose."

The images of motherhood we grew up with often conflict with the day-to-day job of being a mom. Janet says, "My image of the ideal mother is primarily media generated and partly generated by the fact that my mom was a completely calm person. At least that's how she presented herself. So combined with media images of mothers having fun, my mom's calm personality really influenced me. I think the biggest surprise is how hard being a mother is. How completely hard, much harder than I ever imagined taking care of kids could be, both from an emotional standpoint and in terms of all the juggling."

Even though we think we're prepared for mothering a new baby, we may be taken by surprise by the "real thing." Lucy says, "I had this vision of myself being this really chic mom. I'd be well dressed. The baby would be well dressed. The house would be decorated and the baby's room would look like it was right out of a magazine. I'd be rested and perky. I'd have all this time to do all sorts of interesting things. I really thought I'd have a baby and he'd sit on the floor and play with his toys while I made dinner. I don't know what I was thinking. I guess I didn't have any concept of how much work a baby is and how little else I would be able to get done as a new mother."

What Kind of Mother Do I Want to Be?

Naturally many of our ideas about motherhood are based on our own mothers.

Our attitudes about motherhood are shaped by our own childhood memories and by cultural influences. Some of us want to imitate our own mothers and others of us want to be a different kind of parent. But for each of us, our experience of childhood plays a powerful role in how we envision ourselves as moms. Many of us who are having children in our thirties and forties are trying to reconcile the traditional images of motherhood we were raised with and our expectations for our own emotional and personal development. Our goal is to be present and available for our children without sacrificing the sense of mastery and confidence we earned in our postcollege years through our careers. We want to maintain our sense of self but also be attentive parents and partners.

Many of us have a concept of motherhood that focuses on our emotional relationship with our family. Gabrielle says, "My mother was a pretty down-to-earth, involved mom. She went to college, but there was never any question that she would stay home with her kids *when* (not *if*) they came along. Thus I didn't have a whole lot of theoretical images about what mothers should be. Basically I saw myself as a caregiver, educator, nurturer, and, ultimately, 'chopped liver' if I did my job right. My self-image of motherhood did not involve any domestic aspect of 'homemaker.' It was (and is) focused on my relationship with my child and husband, and not my ability to cook, clean, or appear at the door in Saran Wrap and lipstick when my husband comes home from work."

Naturally many of our ideas about motherhood are based on our own mothers. Cynthia feels that her mother's influence is present in both obvious and subtle ways. She says, "My ideal mother is my mother. I don't really compare myself to her on an ongoing basis. I never think, 'What would my mom do in this situation?' because in many ways, I think I do what my mom would do in the situation. I think we are products of our upbringing and a lot of parenting, unfortunately, is unconscious. So to the extent that you were reared well by your parents, you will hopefully do the same by your children. My mom is my role model. When my first daughter was born, I truly felt like a mother and embraced it, because of the example my mom set. Whatever frustrations she may have had with motherhood, she never showed us. It never came out in her mothering. She was always there for us and was very loving."

Some of us may want to be a different kind of mother than our mothers were. Cecily, the mother of a two-year-old, describes how she's trying to remake motherhood in a different image than that of her mother. She believes that her mother put her children first and didn't take her own needs into consideration. She says, "Many of my fears about motherhood had to do with my mother's actualization of the role. She was a nurse before she had young children, and she stayed at home full-time with us until the youngest was in first grade when she went back to work part-time. My mother is the consummate caregiver and sacrificed many of her own needs — financially, emotionally — for those of her children. Although I knew I could fashion the kind of mother I would be from the many wonderful role models I've had over the years, I couldn't ignore the overwhelming impact my mother had on my life. In the end I trusted that I would evolve into my own version of a mother without 'becoming my mother.'"

Sometimes the ways in which we were raised can give us insight into how *not* to raise our own children. Bonnie's goal is to bring her daughter up with a strong sense of self. She says, "My ideal was to not raise my daughter the way I was raised, but to do it differently. The whole thing for me is to do it better and to build my daughter's self-esteem, something I feel that I didn't have. So for me, being a mother was a choice I made with my husband. We wanted to be parents in a way that was psychologically beneficial to our child. That's what keeps me connected to the art of mothering: my wanting to give my daughter a solid sense of self-esteem so when she's my age she will know her own worth."

I'm Not Sure I Feel Like a Mother Yet

Integrating motherhood into who we were before we had children is a process that can be challenging but filled with possibilities for personal growth.

In his work on adult development, Erik Erikson observed that life progresses in stages. Each stage is marked by a turning point or "crisis" that is a crucial period of increased vulnerability and heightened potential.[19] When put in this context, motherhood can be viewed as a passage in which each of us must perform the associated developmental tasks without the techniques that worked for us in our pre-baby life. And because any transition requires that we give up parts of our old life, this passage can be both exciting and difficult.

Integrating motherhood into who we were before we had children is a process that can be challenging but filled with possibilities for personal growth. Particularly in the first few months of motherhood, we struggle with what it means to be a mom. Our lives are so tied to our infant that sometimes it's hard to disassociate from our role as caregiver and remember who we are as a separate person. Author Andrea Boroff Eagan studied what happens psychologically to a new mother during her baby's first nine months. In her book *The Newborn Mother: Stages of Her Growth,* she explains the emotions that new mothers experience and shows that our feelings often follow a predictable pattern.

Eagan found that in the first one to two months of a baby's life, the mother's role is primarily that of a caretaker. We are bound to our baby through physical nurturing. For many mothers, we begin forming a strong emotional attachment when the baby starts responding to us through fixed gazes and intentional smiles. After all, what could be more "validating" as a mom than our infant's first little toothless grin?

In months two through five, as the emotional relationship develops, mothers and children are consumed with each other. Eagan calls this the "symbiotic phase." Developmentally the baby cannot differentiate himself from his mother. Meanwhile, we are falling in love with our infant and are more interested in our baby than anything else. Our own sense of identity can be lost in this symbiotic relationship. Often we describe ourselves in this phase as not knowing who we are or not having an interest in the outside world. Ironically this is the time when maternity leaves end and we are expected to be back to "normal." If we return to work, we have to figure out how to combine the routines and responsibilities of parenthood and work. For those of us who elect to stay home, we must redefine ourselves through our lives as parents rather than through our jobs.

In the fifth month, babies start establishing some independence and we mothers start to turn our attention back to ourselves and to the outside world. By the sixth or seventh month, as the baby's independence increases, we may feel more confident in our mothering skills and less preoccupied with caring for our child. We may start to focus on our lives apart from the baby. We may take steps to reestablish an identity as well as working to get back in shape physically. By the eighth or ninth month, the baby has developed into a clearly separate person who is beginning to explore the world around him or her. Our role begins to shift from nurturer and protector to teacher and playmate. During this time, we may have reconnected with the world and are trying to incorporate motherhood into our ongoing life.[20]

Who Am I?

*Motherhood is much less task oriented than the work world,
and I was untrained for the routine.*

Eagan's work is enlightening because it provides some explanation and precedent for what we may be experiencing in those first nine months. One of the hardest things is to sort out who we are now that we're moms. Although many of us felt a strong bond with our baby right away, most of us don't immediately feel like mothers. Gabrielle talks about the process of forming an identity as a mother and figuring out what a mother does with her time: "Although I began to feel like a mom when I fell in love with my child at five weeks, it took me a long time to feel like I knew how to act like a mom.

I had spent all my life in school and then as a professional, career-oriented worker bee. Despite the fact that I am the product of a stay-at-home mom, I certainly did not see myself as a version of her and I had no idea what a 'mom' did all day."

Gabrielle goes on to say, "When my son was about two months old, I went to visit my sister, a mother of two and several years ahead of me in the mommy game. This visit was extremely helpful to me — seeing how a 'mom' functioned. Motherhood is much less task oriented than the work world, and I was untrained for the routine. Spending time doing the mommy thing with my sister was great — she was incredibly busy and functional. My fears about becoming a TV-addicted hausfrau were allayed. Her mothering role did not preclude relationships with other grown-ups or her involvement in activities in which she was interested. My sister described her job as a mom saying, 'I work with great people, I get tremendous positive feedback from them, I see the results of my work constantly, and it's as challenging as any job I've ever had.' This definitely gave me a perspective and framework for starting to remake myself from career girl to mom."

Experiencing a crisis of identity is not unusual for new moms. Cynthia says she had an identity crisis when her baby was five weeks old. She recalls, "I remember when my first daughter was five weeks old. I hadn't been working, but my whole identity was still as a doctor. Being a doctor was the only thing I ever wanted to be aside from a mother. I was driving in horrible traffic, the baby was crying, and I panicked. I was sweating, and I'm thinking, 'What am I doing?' I didn't know if I was a doctor or a mother or a person or anything. I was really distraught. In hindsight, I would say that my path to motherhood has been a passage. It wasn't an overnight thing where one day I was a doctor and the next day I was a mother. It's been a day-by-day travel, and only with time do I feel that I've fully established my identity as a mother. I'm comfortable in it for now, and I'll have to see how it evolves as my children get older."

Not surprisingly, our baby's temperament plays a role in how we feel about ourselves as mothers. If we have an "easy" baby, we feel more confident in our mothering skills than if we have a baby that presents more challenges. If our babies are more difficult to care for, it may take longer for us to feel comfortable in the maternal role. Laura describes her daughter's first year and how it impacted her view of herself as a mother: "I didn't feel like a mother until I was a year into it. My baby was colicky for a good six to eight months so we had a rough first year. I couldn't get a reaction from her so it was hard to feel bonded. My baby's temperament really affected how I felt about myself as a mom."

Having children in quick succession can also impact our sense of self. Eleanor's life changed dramatically when she had two children in two years. Although delighted with her two children, she's still trying to determine how to define herself as a mother because she finds the role itself is not strictly defined: "My self-image has changed a lot — in some respects, positively and in other respects, negatively. The positive part is that I'm much happier than I thought I would be. Staying home with my two children and watching them grow up has been wonderful. And I have new confidence in an area that I didn't have any experience. The negative part is that how I feel about myself is still not fully formed. Here I went to school and prepared for a career, but I'm not using any of that right now. I don't feel like I prepared as much for being a mother. So although I feel confident about being a mother, I'm still trying to figure out how to be happy with myself as a whole person."

Many of us face the question of how we view ourselves as mothers when our maternity leave ends and we must address the issue of how to combine motherhood and work. Heather, who has a three-month-old, surprised herself by deciding while on maternity leave not to return to job. She says she wondered how she would occupy her time and her mind as an at-home mother, but knows she's made the right decision. She says, "I'm settling into being a mother and am surprised by how happy I am. Happier than I've ever been in fact. This is a part of my identity that was lacking. As a mother, I feel complete."

I'm Surprised by My Body

Although we may have had hopes of returning to our previous size within a few weeks of delivery, it often takes much longer.

Most of us find that being a mother has changed our physical self-image as well as our psychological self. Going through pregnancy, giving birth, and nursing a child are extraordinary events, giving us an appreciation of what our bodies can do. At the same time, many of us are surprised by how much of our self-image is a function of our appearance. Gaining weight is especially unsettling for many women. Even though we know intellectually that putting on additional weight is all part of the process of carrying a child, we may feel upset about "getting fat" and about the changes in our body that remain even after we've given birth.

Although we may have had hopes of returning to our previous size within a few weeks of delivery, it often takes much longer. And even when the scale says we weigh what we did before we were pregnant, the shape of our body is often different. There are some fortunate women who do resume their pre-baby bodies in a month or two, but for many of us, it can take a year to feel like our old selves. This shouldn't be surprising when we consider the length of our pregnancies! To the extent that we focus less on the fact that we may not fit into our favorite blue jeans anytime soon and more on the miracle that we participated in, we'll be happier with our physical selves.

Some of us experience new pride in our bodies. Tina, who has an eight-week-old baby, talks about how awed she is by her body. She says, "My husband thinks I'm the sexiest woman right now. We thought being pregnant was fantastic. When you're pregnant, your body goes through all these great changes over nine months. But when you have the baby, your body experiences so much in just twenty-four hours. It was amazing when my milk came in. We both admired how incredible a mother's body is, so powerful and strong. I felt really proud of myself."

But body changes can also make us wonder who (or where) we are. Leslie talks about how gaining weight during her pregnancy makes her feel like someone other than herself. "What is my self-image right now?" asks Leslie. "Fat. So much of it tied to weight. I gained fifty pounds when I was pregnant. My side of the bed is still a lot heavier than my husband's, and he's a big guy. Since I've had children, I feel matronly. I was a career woman for ten years before I had a baby. So when I became a mom, I didn't know how to dress anymore. I wondered, 'What do mothers wear?' That sounds kind of shallow, but I didn't feel like myself anymore. Sometimes I see a picture of myself and think, 'Is that what I look like now?' It's been a struggle because I feel like the same person in many ways, but physically I look so different."

Our changing bodies can be perplexing. Amy, who had

always been very athletic, was at once delighted and distressed by the physical changes she experienced during pregnancy. She recalls, "I had this blow to my self-confidence when I was expecting because I viewed myself as this big huge woman. That was hard. Also I was used to being so capable and now I had to turn to men on airplanes and say, 'Would you mind putting my bag up on the rack for me?' On the other hand, I do pride myself on being strong and self-sufficient, so I broke all the rules during pregnancy. I traveled until the end of thirty six weeks. I did it my way and that made a big difference to me."

Joyce says that going through two pregnancies and childbirth has made her much more confident about her body: "With each child, I've become more comfortable with my body. The first pregnancy was much harder for me than the second. I've learned to surrender to the changes in my body because I know I can lose the weight and get back in shape. In many ways I feel like I'm healthier now, and I feel better. I've just relaxed more. Both times I went through a pregnancy, I became more familiar with the routine and it was less scary. I stepped back one day and realized that no one is scrutinizing me, so it doesn't matter if I weigh five pounds more than I did before I had children. That's the great secret. We all have to let go and really feel that."

I Feel Better When I Take Care of Myself

Though it can be uncomfortable for some of us to do, asking
for help is one way we can nurture ourselves.

The challenge for new moms is to not become depleted while caring for our baby. And there's little disagreement that we need to take breaks from the constancy of motherhood. Unlike a job where you can go home at the end of the day and "leave it behind," motherhood is an around-the-clock proposition. Therefore it's important to find some time for *us*, even if it's hiring a baby-sitter or coercing a friend into watching our baby for an hour so we can go out and take a walk. Most of us require time alone to rejuvenate. Others of us are refreshed by spending time with our husbands or girlfriends. Whatever it is that allows us to reconnect with our own strength and resources is something we need to make time for on a regular basis.

Each of us has to find her own way of taking care of herself. A mother of two, Joanne gives her prescription for maintaining her sanity: "As we all know, being a mother is totally selfless and all-consuming, so it is in small ways that I try to take care of myself. For example, in the first years of my older son's life, I barely brushed my teeth and washed my face in the morning, until I finally said, 'This is crazy.' So I bought myself some expensive, delicious smelling face creams to cleanse and moisturize with, and I lock myself in the bathroom every morning for a good . . . oh, three and a half minutes, do a home facial, and emerge a new woman, ready to face another day of motherhood. I had also given up a daily paper shortly after my first baby was born, because I just watched them pile up unopened day after day. (I remember calling the paper to cancel it, and when questioned why I was canceling, I almost burst into tears as I explained I'd probably never have a moment to myself for the next ten years!) I now read the *New York Times* seven days a week."

Many of us find the support of others to be necessary and nurturing. Janet has two children and says that one of the things that really helps her keep her balance is participating in a parents' support group: "Taking care of myself enables me to sustain a connection with my husband and with my kids. If I'm feeling bad, then I know I've stored up too many negative feelings to be connected to anyone. My parents' group is a safe place to get it all out."

Though it can be uncomfortable for some of us to do, asking for help is one way we can nurture ourselves. Jenny is the mother of a six-month-old and says she's slowly learning to accept help from others. She observes, "Since becoming a mother I've found ways of caring for myself by letting myself rely on others. This is a new thing for me. After my mother went home and returned to full-time teaching, I had an aunt who offered to come occasionally and baby-sit. My aunt was wonderful, not just for baby-sitting but also for company and advice. A few hours away from my baby make me a more balanced parent."

Work can be an important form of self-nurturance for some new mothers. Deborah, a single mother and a management consultant, finds that working provides a different kind of gratification than that she gets from child rearing. She states, "I don't do that much to take care of myself. I put my career in that category because it gives me a lot of satisfaction. I don't have baby-sitters on weekends. I don't want to do that, although it is hard to go get my hair cut. But I do have a regular Wednesday night baby-sitter. That's one night a week that I know I can work late or go to a movie. I've never gone away on a trip, other than a business trip, without my son. When I do travel for business, I really savor the time on the airplane, read magazines, have breakfast in bed in the morning. Because there's so little of it, I really take advantage of it. The truth of the matter is that I get so much joy out of my son that I don't feel the need to go off and get a daylong massage."

Most of us know that exercise (and pushing a stroller to Starbuck's *does* count) produces psychological as well as physical benefits. Plus, doing some form of physical activity on a regular basis may give us a sense of control in the otherwise unpredictable world of babies and small children. A working mother, Elise views going to the gym twice a week as her "salvation." She says, "Exercise for me is a really important part of coping. In fact, I notice a real difference if I don't exercise. I feel like a load is taken off me when I'm able to work out even if only twice a week."

The supportive environment of a local gym can add to the physical rewards of exercise. Cynthia says, "I exercise as much as I can. Of course it's never consistent because it depends on what's happening in the rest of my life. I have a real support system at the gym. Over the years I've been going there, I've met these women friends and we've all had babies together. We've all supported each other through our pregnancies and births as our bodies have gotten big then small again. Most of the women are going there for peace of mind and a sense of doing something for themselves, not vanity. It's a way to keep ourselves sane."

The challenge is to give our children what they need while holding onto those parts of ourselves that make us who we are. In other words, mothers of small children must "mother" themselves occasionally. We need to rest and take time for ourselves so that we are not exhausted physically and emotionally. In caring for ourselves, we have more love and energy to give to our baby.

I'm Becoming a Different Person

Through motherhood, we grow and grow and grow some more.

Becoming a mother forces us to enlarge our self-image as we incorporate our parental identity and responsibilities into our old lives. And motherhood can provide us with fresh insight into ourselves if we are willing to change with the new role. As psychologist Lucy Scott writes, "Motherhood is an opportunity to confront our fears and dreams and to discover new possibilities for commitment and personal growth."[21] Betsy views motherhood as a continuous opportunity to learn about herself. She says, "Motherhood for me is a constant process of self-reflection. The way I treat my children, react to them, teach them, talk to them, think about them has taught me more about myself than I ever imagined. Never in my life have I been forced to look at who I am so intensely and honestly. Mothering has brought out the best in me and the worst in me. It has made me truly realize what is important in life."

Through motherhood, we grow and grow and grow some more. Megan, who has a one-year-old son, writes, "I think the journey into motherhood is not a linear process where birth, growth, and development can be crossed off like tasks completed. I seem to cover the same ground over and over with constant periods of intense joy mixed with sleep deprivation, anxiety, and concern. There are longer periods of quiet between. My days are no longer matters of just coping but are filled with gladness, self-confidence, and hope. The first year of my son's life has passed so quickly that I realize the importance of not just planning for the future but being present in the moment, where I am and where our family is."

With time we weather the transition in identity and eventually may feel like ourselves again. Rosemary, a mother of three, says, "When I was in my twenties, I was pretty wild and independent. I worked hard, explored a lot of new things, and constantly tested the limits. But now that I'm a mother, I realize that the life I was living then was pretty distant from who I really am. As a mother I'm a lot closer to the person I was when I was growing up, because I'm putting my true beliefs and values into practice every day."

Sometimes we simply need to get back to the self who was always there. Now the mother of four, Caroline says, "It was hard on my self-image becoming a mother. I originally lamented all the things I was giving up. I thought, 'I'll never ride my bike again. I'll never have sex again. I'll never have a private moment again. I'll never *fill-in-the-blank* again.' I had the bad idea that I would be totally one with my baby and become someone totally different as a mom. The truth is that you should never go away from yourself. You've got to be who you always were. You can't be a different mother, wife, or person than you are. And the reward is that as your kids get older, they start appreciating you in spite of all of your weird personality quirks."

For most of us, being a new parent is challenging, gratifying, and not at all like we expected. Instead of assuming that we'll know how to be a mom right from the start, we must give ourselves time to grow into the role and be open to the opportunities for change that parenthood offers. One of the early lessons our babies teach us is that it's impossible to be a perfect mom. Instead of aspiring to an ideal, we must simply try to meet most of our children's needs most of the time, without losing touch with ourselves. The compensation for discovering that we aren't fantasy moms is the realization that our babies love us anyway, imperfections and all.

THREE

How Do I Integrate My Professional Self with Motherhood?

Straddling two worlds is like riding two horses. If I can just head them both in the same direction, then I won't be torn apart.

— Beth Wilson Saavedra

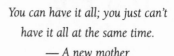

You can have it all; you just can't
have it all at the same time.
— A new mother

The women's movement has changed the landscape for today's mothers. To work or not to work is *the* question for those of us who pursued careers in our twenties and are having babies in our thirties and forties. Since the 1970s, record numbers of women have been entering the workforce and laboring in better-paying jobs (many of which had traditionally been held by men). And unlike women in previous generations, most of us don't think of ourselves solely as wives and mothers. Many of us also have professional identities that bring us a sense of mastery and satisfaction.

Having worked for many years before having a baby, we are making a spectrum of choices about how to combine motherhood and employment. In addition to full-time jobs, some of us are working flexible schedules, part-time or out of the home. There are others of us who have quit our jobs to stay home but are using our professional skills to start independent businesses or participate in civic or volunteer activities. But our quest to achieve the right balance for our family is an ongoing process. Or as Louise puts it, "I know very few mothers, no matter what their decision about work, who don't continue to think about it. Everyone thinks about it even if they're happy with the choices they've made. There are times when we all ask, 'Did I make the right choice for me and my family? Am I doing what I chose to do well?'"

Too often we feel guilty about our decisions — in large part because in our culture, it is primarily mothers who are held accountable for how our children "turn out." We're caught in a double bind: wanting to be "good mothers" but also feeling pressure to "use" our education and training to accomplish something professionally. Ultimately the decisions about how we balance work and family are individual ones, made according to each of our personal, professional, and financial circumstances.

Although it would have been neater, I resisted the temptation to divide this chapter into one about working mothers and one about at-home mothers. That kind of separation does a disservice to all of us, since many of the issues we new mothers face are similar. As older mothers, most of us have had serious careers before having children and appreciate the benefits and stresses of paid employment. This professional experience informs how we feel about combining work with motherhood, regardless of whether we decide to continue working or to stay home or to do some combination of both. Since I became a mother, I've been lucky enough to work outside the home, to stay at home, and to work from home. I know from experience that the concerns of working and non-working mothers aren't always the same, yet each of us is trying to do what is "best" for our family.

What makes it tricky is that there is no consensus on

what the "best" course is. Although social scientists have been researching the effects of work on mothers and families for years, the findings are inconclusive. There is a credible study to validate whatever decision we make. Rather than feeling insecure about our decisions or second-guessing the choices that other women make, we must decide what is right for us at a given point in time and revisit the work/family balance as our circumstances evolve.

And instead of separating into two camps, we need to support each other's choices and together elevate the status and value of raising children in our culture.

I'm Working Outside the Home

For many of us, our work is a big part of who we are.

The majority of mothers in the U.S. work outside the home. In 1998, 65 percent of us with children age five and under worked, and 75 percent of all mothers worked.[22] We work because we have established ourselves in our careers, and our families depend on our income. As women who have worked several years before becoming mothers, we may not want to leave our jobs and give up our reputation, expertise, and contacts — not to mention our salaries. Having derived satisfaction from our careers, some working mothers wonder if we would be happy staying at home. We find that working can fulfill our intellectual and creative impulses as well as providing social benefits. By earning a paycheck, we feel more independent and in control. We believe we are being good role models to our children by having a separate identity outside the home. And when we can find good child care, we feel that our children gain from having other loving adults in their lives.

For many of us, our work is a big part of who we are. A marketing executive and mother of a two-year old, Elaine can't imagine what her life would be like without her job. She says, "I like the identity and strength I gain from being part of an exciting business. I like the recognition and being part of something meaningful to me and to others. Using my brain every minute of the day energizes me. I wonder if I would be a good mom if I stayed at home and didn't work outside the home. It's how I judge myself. I don't think I'd be as good a mom or as full a person. Maybe I'm just so busy right now that I can't think about it. But I get a panicked feeling when I ask myself, 'What if I didn't work someday?'"

How we perceive ourselves as working moms can change as our child changes. Teresa has an eighteen-month-old and a demanding job as an investment banker. She wouldn't dream of giving up her professional life right now. She describes her evolution as a working mom: "Before I had the baby, I worried about how I would continue to work, but I never seriously thought I'd stay home. Part of it is that I like my work. Part of it is financial. And part of it is that my husband and I feel if there's a time for us to work hard, it's now. Our son's needs are pretty straightforward right now and can be met by a good caretaker. We feel that as he gets older, there will be more critical periods in his life when we'll absolutely have to be there."

As her son has moved out of the baby phase, Teresa has been able to sharpen her focus at work. She says, "I think I'm more confident about my job because I'm a mother. The same attention to detail I pour into my child, I put into my job. And some of the neurotic energy that went into my job now goes to my child so they both benefit. When I first got back from maternity leave, work was really hard. I didn't feel like I was really there. I was nursing and dragging a lot. But I thought, no matter how bad my day gets at work, five minutes away there's this great kid of mine." She continues, "But at twelve months when I was weaning and starting to get some perspective, I began thinking that I really wanted more from work. Being a mom made me focus. I could distill out the noise and concentrate on what was important. The most annoying thing about being a working mom is that I'm on a schedule. I have to be home at x hour and I have y number of things that need to get done at work. So I have to be very directed. Being a mother has made me much more efficient. I'm a better employee for it."

Some of us love the sense of personal fulfillment that work provides us and are resolved about our choices. Victoria has worked for almost twenty years in the publishing industry. She says, "I work because of the stimulation and personal growth I experience. If I get to a point where I'm not growing anymore, then I'll find other things to do that make me grow. That's my primary motivator and, of course, I like the compensation. I'm the kind of person who gets easily resolved about my decisions, period. And when my children need a little more of me, I don't feel guilty because that's just the trait of a child. A child will always ask us for more, even if you're an at-home mom. Even on those days when my boss is on a rampage, my kids fall apart when I get home, and my husband is in a bad mood, even when it gets that bad, I don't second-guess myself. I know there are going to be bad days, but they always blow over and we get back on course."

I Didn't Know My Maternity Leave Would End So Quickly

As we contemplate our return to the workforce, we're not really sure how we're going to combine the demands of a career and parenthood.

Many of us find returning to our job after maternity leave is extremely difficult. We're just starting to get the hang of motherhood, and now we're expected to add work back into our demanding new schedule. Who would have imagined how complicated the logistics of returning to our job could be? And what mother feels happy about leaving her precious baby with a relative stranger? We wonder how anyone or any organization could ever be loving, responsible, and caring enough to take care of *our child*. On the other hand, we may be eager to return to a setting that's familiar, where we can have uninterrupted conversation with other adults and over which we have some control. As we contemplate our return to the workforce, we're not really sure how we're going to combine the demands of a career and parenthood.

Often we have contradictory feelings about the choices we have to make. Megan talks about going back to her teaching job after a twelve-week maternity leave: "I was happy going to work until I actually got to work, and then I was miserable. I was tied up from nine to twelve each morning, and by the time class ended I felt like my breasts were about to burst. Students would approach me after class to ask questions or schedule appointments, and I, who had always been so accommodating and approachable, would dismiss them abruptly and run down the hall as fast as I could to my office and my waiting breast pump. I couldn't give up breast-feeding because it was so important to me to feel like my son wasn't being cared for differently since I had returned to my job. I felt better because breast milk was still something no one could give him but me. I would sit at work and think about my baby and be consumed with longing for him. Then I would race home to relieve the baby-sitter and start worrying about all the things I had failed to accomplish at work. I felt like I was never content but always wanting to be where I was not."

For many moms, intellectual stimulation is an important reason to return to our jobs. Heidi has five-month-old twins. She was happy to return to full-time work at a law firm after a three-month maternity leave because she missed using her mind. She explains, "I wasn't sure how I would feel until after I had the babies, but I was committed to coming back to work and seeing whether I could handle it. It took me the first four weeks of my maternity leave to relax. I found that it took those four weeks to get used to the idea of being a mom, to get into the babies' schedule, and to take pleasure in the experience rather than dreading it. During the middle four weeks of my maternity leave, I started feeling like things were getting a little less crazy, and my body was starting to return to normal. Then in the last four weeks of my leave, I had to hire a baby-sitter and start thinking about going back to work. But as it got closer and closer, I was okay about it. I felt like I had a good bond with the babies. I loved them and I knew they loved me. I didn't have any anxiety that I was going to leave and they would forget who I was. And I really wanted to get my brain back."

Heidi goes on to say, "The turning point was going to a dinner party when the twins were two months old. I'd been on bedrest for a month before they were born, so it had been three months since I'd met a new person. At this dinner, I was seated next to a fellow who could have been a good business contact for me. And I couldn't put two sentences together. I couldn't explain what I did. It was really frightening actually.

That was the signal to me that I needed to get back into the flow of things. That helped me get excited about coming back to work. So far, it's working out well."

Some of us know *for certain* that we'll go back to work after we become mothers — and are surprised when we start feeling *uncertain* about our intentions. Heather always thought she would be a working mom, but decided during her maternity leave that she wanted to stay home with her baby. She describes how her pre-baby beliefs were challenged by the presence of a real live child: "Before I had a baby, I was guilty of believing that if you were a smart woman with skills that of course you would go back to work. That's what I thought the feminist model expected. My desire to work and the assumption that I would work was driven by the feminist ideology I prescribed to. So deciding not to return to work was a difficult decision for me, because I always thought I would work outside the home. A lot of it was that I did not want to be anything remotely like my mother. So I am letting go of that fear. And then there was my fear of poverty. I've always wanted to be in control of the money making. So I am trying to let go of my fear and my need to control. In a way it is all very liberating."

There's Not Enough of Me to Go Around

And for many of us, the work/family balance is not resolved quickly or easily.

The hardest thing for most of us who are working mothers is that we always feel stretched. Instead of one demanding job, we now have two. Studies show that the average working mother spends eighty-five hours a week on her job, children, and homemaking. So in addition to forty hours of paid employment, we typically devote forty-five hours a week to our family and home. In effect, this constitutes a "second shift" that is performed by working mothers *after* we leave our jobs and go home at the end of the day.[23]

Before having a baby, if we needed to stay late or work on the weekend to finish a project, we did. But as parents, our time is precious. Many of us feel guilt and frustration about not being able to be a parent or an employee at 100 percent capacity. And in their research on new parents, Cowan and Cowan found that even when employed mothers are content with their lives, not one of the women in the study was entirely satisfied that she was devoting enough energy to her work or that she had chosen the best way to be with her baby.[24] Basically, being a working mother is a constant juggling act.

Stephanie, a lesbian mother of a two-year-old, talks about the formidable task of balancing work and family: "The most challenging thing about being a parent is that it constricts your ability to play any other role. I often feel like I'm not being a very good partner, a very good parent, or a very good boss — that everything suffers by some percentage. That's pretty much the way I feel all the time. I rarely feel like I'm doing my job at 100 percent, being a partner in an adult relationship at 100 percent or being a parent at 100 percent. There's so much to juggle and so many challenges to be a parent and work full-time that I don't think you can do anything at the level of perfection — certainly not at the level you think you'd like to be able to obtain — because it's too demanding. I have to struggle not to be overly critical of myself about all the things that aren't going to get done, because everything is not going to get done. There are just too many demands."

When we have children, our priorities inevitably — and of necessity — change. Megan, an educator with a one-year-old son, reflects on how hard it was to return to work and to realize that where she ranked her job in importance had changed: "The adjustment for me was demoting work in my list of priorities. In the past if I didn't manage my time well, if someone wanted to discuss something late in the afternoon, or if something came up unexpectedly, I would stay as late as I had to, take work home, or come in on the weekend. As a mom, I couldn't do that. Now work had to fit into the discrete time period I had carved out for it. I couldn't dawdle to chat with people on my way out; I couldn't stay late and rewrite a memo that didn't please me. Working at home was impossible now. I would look at the pile of paper I hadn't gotten to and feel guilty. I would be mad at myself for not getting it done, mad at my job for spilling over into my home life, and jealous of my husband who could stay at work as long as he needed to even though I didn't want to stay at work until all hours anymore. At least I thought I didn't. I wanted to be just as productive at work as I had always been but spend lots of time at home with my son. I had to accept the fact that I couldn't have it both ways."

And for many of us, the work/family balance is not resolved quickly or easily. MaryAnne has worked for a foundation for over ten years and has two daughters. She enjoys her job but finds it harder and harder to reconcile her "work self" and her "home self." She says, "I work four days a week and that's doable for me. As a working mom, the hardest part is that basically I do my job and see my family. I don't have time for much of anything else. And as long as everything is going according to plan, everything is fine. But if something throws me off (like my baby getting sick), everything is thrown out of whack. I find it difficult when I'm home to think about work because I want to devote myself 100 percent to my child and to think only about "home" things. At home, there's a totally different pace and set of priorities. My whole tempo is different. So if I have to talk to my boss or make a work-related phone call, I feel pulled in two different directions. I like my work but find that part of it really frustrating."

I'm the One Making Career Concessions

As hard as it can be, we need to remember that choosing to do something now doesn't mean we can't do something else later.

Until men's roles and expectations change, women will continue to have primary responsibility for the home and children. More often than not, we as mothers are making the adjustments in our careers to accommodate the needs of our families. This is in part because of social expectations, and in part because we may not want to relinquish the role of principal parent. Practically speaking, it's difficult to combine two high-powered careers and a family. Many of us have reduced our commitment to our jobs out of necessity so we can be available when our children need us. Although some of us resent that we've had to make career adjustments, others among us choose willingly to scale back (at least for some period of time) so we can be more involved in child rearing. Those of us who work full-time tend to share more parenting responsibilities with our husbands. Even so, as Arlie Hochschild discovered in her study of working parents, we're the ones who actually manage the household and child-care arrangements even when our husbands are pitching in.[25]

The choices we make about our family life impact our work life. Antonia is a lawyer and mother of two. She recounts the changes she made in her career to accommodate her family: "When my first child was a year and a half, I took a more low-key job. I had been working at a large firm and was proud to be there, but I was working long hours and there was no balance in my life. I left that firm for a less demanding job. It was the right thing to do for my family and my marriage, but it set me back career-wise. The law looks down on less prestigious places. I had to go through a series of other jobs to start rebuilding my career after having kids."

Antonia says that her husband has made changes in his life as well: "I'm not the only one who has made concessions. My working has put a lot of responsibility on my husband to take care of the kids. He does 50 percent of the child care and household responsibilities. He gives up a lot of his free time to be with them. We've given up different things. I realize that instead of looking for the perfect title, we're all looking for a happy life."

Though we may make career concessions, we aren't always happy about it. Lucy, a part-time video producer and mother of a thirteen-month-old, says she was prepared to be the one making changes in her professional life but still finds it hard at times. She observes, "I was happy to not work full-time after having a baby, but I also thought it would be more doable to work part-time. I think it's really hard. I can see why I'm the one that needs to make concessions because I don't have the potential to earn the kind of money my husband does. So if we're talking about working because that's what supports the family, then yes, it makes sense that he's the primary worker. But if you look at work as a way to meet other interesting people and to challenge yourself, then I sometimes feel slighted. But I know I'm romancing and simplifying what my husband does because there's a lot of pressure on him as the main breadwinner."

Lucy goes on to say, "Every now and then I miss the commitment that it takes to do interesting work. I can make money working part-time, but I can't really get better at what I'm doing. I can't get the really interesting projects. Although I miss that kind of interesting work, I can't go back to that life. We've all worked so hard to get where we were in our careers and we've just had to let it go as mothers. Our husbands haven't had to do that when they became parents. I think about that."

As mothers, what we give (and give up) is perceived differently that what our husbands give (and give up) as parents. MaryAnne has two children and has reduced her work schedule, while her husband works full-time. She says, "My husband and I have talked about both changing our schedules so that we each work four days a week. I think it's important to make decisions together about work. But in the end, he decided he gets a lot of psychic and intellectual benefits from his job and is not as interested in staying home with the kids as I am. So he continues to work full-time and I'm the one scaling back. There's a lot of pressure on us moms. For instance, any involvement my husband has with the kids is perceived as great, whereas any time I spend away from my kids (like an overnight business trip) is viewed as suspect."

As hard as it can be, we need to remember that choosing to do something now doesn't mean we can't do something else later. Louise discusses how her job choices in her marketing career have tracked events in her family's life: "I geared when I worked more and when I worked less to what was going on in my children's lives — their births, their starting school, and so on. My husband didn't do that. I guess it depends on how much energy you have and where you want to put it. To me it's important to spend time with my children and to have fun with them. I'm fortunate because I found work that is interesting but doesn't rule my life. Trying to strike the balance is the big challenge for me. My mom says that you're going to live a long life and you can do a variety of things. Doing something now doesn't have to foreclose options at points down the road. Hopefully I'll have thirty or forty more productive years and I'll do lots of different things during that time."

I Couldn't Do This without Good Child Care

Each child care arrangement must be evaluated on its own merits and in relation to each family's unique needs.

Whether we choose to stay home or choose to go back to work, no mother relishes the thought of leaving her child with someone else. In a country where there is little institutional support for raising children, each new family must put together its own piecemeal solution to child care. For women who return to work, the process of finding a satisfactory day-care arrangement or baby-sitter can be daunting. Having never required child care before, we aren't sure how to assess our options. And since many of us grew up in a time where the majority of mothers didn't work, we can't count on traditional values or our own experience for direction.[26] Each child care arrangement must be evaluated on its own merits and in relation to each family's unique needs. When we are comfortable with our arrangement, we feel confident about our child's well-being and can focus on our work.

Finding good child care is never simple. Aliza has a one-month-old and plans to return to her work at a federal agency when her baby is three months old. She says, "Before I had the baby, I didn't think I would be so worried about arranging child care, but now I'm overwhelmed. My son is so young, I can't imagine leaving him at all. I didn't know how vulnerable a small baby would be. There's a day-care center near my office so I went to look at it. I was torn because it felt kind of institutional, although it would be great to have him so close by. But thinking about hiring a baby-sitter is tough too. How can I be sure that I can find someone trustworthy and responsible? Baby-sitters aren't accredited like day-care facilities."

How do we find someone we trust to look after our baby? Megan talks about how difficult it was to interview baby-sitters for the first time: "I was in denial up until a few weeks before I returned to work about the fact that I was going to go back. I put off hiring a baby-sitter until the last possible moment because the act of interviewing potential sitters would make me realize too clearly that I was going to pay a stranger to watch my son. I never did figure out what the appropriate questions were to ask during the job interview. Friends suggested that I ask how the sitter would spend a typical day. 'How do I spend a typical day?' I wondered. I try to keep my son happy and pray that he will take a nap. 'Ask what the sitter would do if the baby got sick while you were at work,' suggested another friend. The baby might get sick? I panicked. That's it. I definitely can't go back to work."

As much as we hope to find "Mary Poppins," we may feel unhappy when we do. Megan talks about the tension of wanting your child to have good rapport with the care provider but at the same time envying the budding relationship with someone else: "I hired a wonderful woman who had grown children of her own and had been caring for young children for ten years. I was not prepared for the adjustment of bringing a baby-sitter into our family. I had arranged for the baby-sitter to start work the week before I returned to work so that I could get comfortable with her and she could get comfortable with our son, our house, and our family. A good baby-sitter develops an independent relationship with your child, but it was painful for me to watch it happen. I hated being in the house trying to prepare for work and hearing the baby-sitter and my son playing downstairs. The first day the baby-sitter left to take our son to the park, I had to exercise all my self-control not to follow them down the street. I was happy going to work at last because I was so unhappy hanging around at home watching the stranger I was paying fall in love with my child."

Some of us choose day care over a baby-sitter because of its reliability. A sales manager, Paula sends her three-year-old and one-and-a-half-year-old to a day care near her home. She says, "My children go to day care because I thought it was a more stable option than hiring a baby-sitter. My husband and I both have demanding jobs, and we needed child care that was absolutely dependable. My children enjoy it because they get to be around children who are older and younger than they are. Also, the center is creative and innovative; they are always thinking about interesting things to do with the kids. The time I spend with my children is pretty low-key. We read; we play; we talk. So all the activities they do during the day take some of the pressure off me to do those things when I get home from work. I initially worried that they wouldn't get enough one-on-one time, but seeing how much they enjoy going, I know they're getting a lot of love and attention."

I'm Home So I Can Be with My Baby

Being at home with our children requires both flexibility and structure.

How do women who have worked all of their adult lives make the transition to being at-home mothers? Although many of us always wanted to be moms, few of us aspired to be house-wives. We've had to reconcile the traditional role of mother with our coming of age in the feminist era and the self-esteem we earned in the workplace. Most older women who stay home have worked and probably will work again. Often we view this time at home as one of many phases in our lives. We have decided to stay home so we will have the time and energy to be emotionally available to our children and part-ners. We have the freedom to make our own schedules and (to some degree) pursue our own interests. Some of us take pleasure in creating a comfortable home environment and in investing in the local community. As the authors of the book *Lifeprints* observe, the role of full-time mother seems to work best for those of us who have made a conscious decision that, at least for the time being, we best meet our own needs and our family's needs by being at home.[27]

Staying at home can cause us to reevaluate our career needs and options. Eve has a business degree and worked in brand management before having her first child. She says she expects more from a job now that she has children, because of the sacrifices required to be a working mother. She says, "After I had my baby and was trying to evaluate what to do career-wise, I came up with four requirements for a job. First, I had to feel challenged by the work and that I was learning from it. Second, I had to feel like I was contributing something that mattered, either by adding to the bottom line or providing a social service. Third, the environment had to be nice and I had to enjoy the people. Finally, it had to be worthwhile financially. When I realized that my current job didn't meet all the requirements, I decided to stay home. I knew that if the job didn't meet those standards, I'd rather be at the playground with my son."

Motherhood becomes a career for some of us. Leslie has two sons, ages three and one. Before she became a mother, she worked for ten years in the textile industry. She quit when she got pregnant because her job involved so much cross-country travel. She says, "I'm really happy to be a mother. I was a very one-dimensional person as a career woman. It was my total identity. I have something to give the world and right now, I'm giving it to my children. Someday I'll go back to work, but I don't feel the need to get back into the corporate world. I love my freedom. I love being able to set my own schedule and be with my children when it's important and have the flexibility to travel. Right now being a mother is my career."

Being at home with our children requires both flexibility and structure. Rosemary was on the partnership track at a law firm when she left her job to be home full-time after she had her second baby. She loves having the flexibility to spend time with her children, yet notes the importance of creating structure in her family's life. She says, "I left my job because I just didn't want to miss out. I wanted to be there for my children. One of the adjustments for me is discovering that as a stay-at-home mother, there is only structure in your day to the extent that you impose it. Otherwise all your time is spent being responsive to other people's needs. While in an office you can focus on one thing, the nature of a mother's job is doing lots of small tasks simultaneously. For my own sanity, I've had to set goals and create structure so I feel like I have some control in my life as a stay-at-home mom."

Even with its drawbacks, being an at-home mom has its rewards. Dana decided to quit working and go back to graduate school while she had a baby so she could spend more time with her daughter as a young child. She says, "One thing I love about being the mom is being the boss. I love being in charge. Having had that kind of flexibility in my life would make it hard to go back and be part of an organization again. I took a lot of satisfaction in the fact that my daughter was growing so well and all she was eating was breast milk, and it was coming from me, only from me. I always felt that was a reward. And having a happy baby was wonderful feedback. I was getting responses from my daughter that made me feel like I was doing a good job as a mother."

How Do I Value Myself As a Mother?

For many of us, there is a tension between our love and
responsibility to our children and the expectation that we will
use the skills and education we acquired in our pre-baby years
in our post-baby lives.

But even if we've made the decision willingly to stay home, much of our identity may continue to be bound up in our jobs. We pride ourselves on the expertise, level of compensation, and reputation that we established in our careers. Thus, the transition from paid work to a more family-centered life can be difficult. Although we are grateful to be able to stay at home, we don't like the loss of status and earning power we associate with being employed. For many of us, there is a tension between our love and responsibility to our children and the expectation that we will use the skills and education we acquired in our pre-baby years in our post-baby lives. In contrast to the structure and feedback that the workplace offers, we may feel that we're not sure how we're doing as a mom because the standards are unclear and we're not sure how to measure our "performance." And because our professional skills, achievements, and ambition don't just disappear when we become stay-at-home mothers, we need to come up with new ways to value ourselves and our work as moms.

The initial transition from career woman to stay-at-home

mother can be a tough one. At age thirty-eight, Veronica had spent sixteen years in the workforce before having a baby. She describes how hard it was to have her identity be that of a mother rather than of a professional: "After I had my first son, I would find myself trying to explain who I was in a very defensive way. I would meet someone new and say, 'I'm a mother, but I used to be a securities trader.' I finally realized that I didn't have to do that because I didn't have to justify my existence as 'just' being a mom."

The sometimes mundane routine of mothering may leave us wondering just how fulfilling our "mom work" is. Serena worked in finance after going to business school. Even though she adored her baby, she sometimes questioned her decision to stay home. She says, "It was a double whammy because I was most paranoid when I was first home with my baby. I couldn't really do much with him except change him and nurse him and sort of play with him. I accomplished something because my child was happy at the end of the day, but sometimes I hadn't even brushed my teeth. It's funny, because I loved being with my son right from the start. It was more about me and my expectations. I remember talking to other moms in the park who thought it was great to not work and felt good about their decision."

Serena continues, "Meanwhile, I felt like I was losing it, that I wasn't *doing* anything. Sometimes it seemed that there were no rewards for being a stay-at-home mom. I wondered why had I gone to school all those years to do this. I thought that I must not be doing it right because I was not happy. At some point, I talked to a friend who put things in perspective for me. She said, 'You're not going to be home forever. Not many people get a five-year 'vacation' from work. It's your time to be in charge so savor it.' It sounds trite, but it was a revelation to me to think about it that way. It took a year and a half, but now I feel good about being at home. And now I realize that you can't seek external feedback. You aren't going to get a good review or a big bonus or whatever. Your kids don't say, 'Great job today, Mom.' You learn to find internal satisfaction for what you're doing."

Though we may not realize it, what we do every day is to nurture new lives. Cynthia went back and forth about her decision to stop working but is grateful that she's been able to spend so much time with her children. She offers, "I put a big value on motherhood and I feel really blessed that I can stay home. Whoever is around your children the most is going to affect them the most. Raising children is a huge responsibility. I've taken on that responsibility and value it. I want to produce good human beings. That in and of itself is of huge value to society because we want people in the world who treat others with respect and fairness. I feel really good about that."

Ironically, valuing ourselves as mothers sometimes means valuing the parts of us that don't have anything to do with motherhood. Joan is getting a second degree so she can change careers. A stay-at-home mother, she believes it is important to have interests beyond her family. She says, "Being a mother is fulfilling in a very nurturing and emotional kind of way. I find great joy in being around my kids and watching them grow. I love every little accomplishment from holding a spoon to tying a shoe. But for me, fulfillment comes in a lot of different ways that don't always involve kids. I do some volunteer work and I find a different kind of fulfillment that way, such as being appreciated more for my skills and my intelligence than for my ability to discipline well. It's important and I want my kids to grow up to be good people, but I don't get all my satisfaction from being a parent. Kids need to see that even at-home moms have other things in their lives besides folding the laundry and going to the park."

We Want to Feel Financially Secure

Our change in earning status often requires that we negotiate new arrangements with our partners to ensure that we don't feel financially vulnerable.

Whether we're home with children or laboring in the workforce, we're concerned about our financial security. And because we worked before having children, we're used to getting paid for our efforts. We like being compensated for a job well done and enjoy the independence that making our own money allows. Women who work feel that it's important to get a paycheck and to know they can provide for their children. We feel a sense of control when we are earning an income.

Women who stay home often feel uncomfortable not contributing to the family's finances. As women who have supported ourselves through our work, it can be scary to become dependent on our husband's salary. And it feels strange to be constantly writing checks (as the person at home managing the household) while not making any money ourselves. Our change in earning status often requires that we negotiate new arrangements with our partners to ensure that we don't feel financially vulnerable. And some of us who are at home have made an effort to keep up our job skills so when we do go back to work, we're not professional dinosaurs.

For some of us, caring for our families includes providing for them financially. Antonia is a lawyer who has worked full-time ever since she had her first child. Now the mother of two, she describes how important it is for her to know she can support her children. She says, "Being a working mother defines my parenthood. I never considered not working. A big part of it was financial. I have this fear that I won't have enough money. By working, I feel that I'm providing for my family. My anxiety comes from feeling like I won't be able to give them what they need. I want to have enough money to do things like provide them with a good education without ending up in debt."

A strong need to be financially independent keeps many of us working. MaryAnne has two daughters ages three and one, and works part-time. She says, "A big part of my working is financial. Earning my own salary makes a big difference in my sense of security. I've realized it's not about the money per se, but it's about my feeling secure and being able to make a contribution to our family, regardless of what my husband makes. I wonder if I didn't work how it might change my relationship with my husband. My parents are divorced so it's important to me to know I have something of my own in case anything happened. It comes down to my having a hard time being in a financially dependent situation."

Our change in financial status affects our husbands as well as us. Shannon wonders how she and her husband will maintain parity in their relationship now that she's decided to quit working to stay at home with their six-month-old daughter. She says, "My husband and I met at graduate school and do similar kinds of work, so we relate as friends. I always brought in a good salary and liked the equality between us. I still haven't figured out how my not working is going to affect our relationship. I don't want the power to change when I stop working. I may be unrealistic, but I expect to be treated the same way even though I'm not making money anymore. My husband will be the primary earner, but I know I could be earning money if I needed to. Actually I think our relationship will get better with my not working because we'll be under less pressure than when both of us were in demanding jobs."

Pressure on our relationship may increase when we quit our job in order to stay home with our children. Linda worked as an architect before becoming a mother. With a four-year-old and a two-year-old, she describes how hard it is not to be a financial contributor anymore. She says, "The impact of having a baby on my relationship with my husband was huge, like being hit by a bomb! There's a level of tension that wasn't there before. It's hard on him that I'm not working and that the entire financial burden for our family is on his shoulders. And my worth went down in the marriage when I stopped working to stay home with the kids. I didn't have the dollars to back me up. It's a terrible feeling. It was something I didn't bargain for. And my husband isn't the one saying, 'You really need a break. Take more money,' so I've learned I have to do that for myself."

An at-home mother of two, Lindsey says that she has to make sure her husband understands her work as a mom and doesn't take her for granted because she's not earning a salary. She says, "At one point, I had to say to my husband, 'You go into an office and manage that office and you get a paycheck for doing those things. My job is to be a mother and I manage the children and the household. And by the way, I don't get paid so it would be nice if you told me 'thank you' every now and then. So I've found that if I check in from time to time, then I don't feel resentment about not being paid for my work, and my husband has an appreciation for what I'm doing for the family."

Do All Mothers Feel Guilty?

It's hard to find the balance. It's not hard to be a parent, but it's hard to do it well.

What is it about mothers and guilt? Even when we're reasonably satisfied with the choices we've made about work and family, there are times when we question whether we are doing the right thing. Mothers who have elected to stay home feel guilty about not always being perfect mothers since we have foregone paid work to be with our children full-time. We envy working mothers for their ability to go to an office and make phone calls without someone pulling on their leg. Working mothers feel guilty that we are not spending as much time with our children as we "should." We're jealous of the stay-at-home mom's ability to pick up in the middle of the day and go to story hour at the library.

Our self-judgment comes from a culture in which we as mothers are assumed to be responsible for our children's wellbeing and in which our children are perceived as reflections of ourselves. With our insecurity comes the impulse to justify our choices and judge those who've made different decisions. But as Michaels and McCarty observe in their book *Solving the Work/Family Puzzle*, "If your priorities reflect your values and the time spent in each of your roles reflects your priorities, you are less likely to suffer role conflicts and the guilt that results." Rather than constantly having an attack of the "guilts," the authors suggest that we analyze whether the cause of our guilt is real or imagined. If there's truly a problem, we need to fix it, and if it's an imagined concern, we should dismiss it.[28]

When a mother works full-time, she may wonder if she is giving up too much by not being with her children, especially when they are very young. Amy says, "I work because I need to. But I have these internal battles about whether I'm abdicating a real responsibility to raise my child to be a secure person. I wonder whether I should ease up right now or work really hard and make some money so I can put it away and not have to worry about it so much. If I do that, will I be giving up too much with my child? Having a child is a wonderful thing. You don't get opportunities this wonderful very often. Yet you still have to keep living your life and making money and working on your marriage and being a good friend to people and having a social life. It's hard to find the balance. It's not hard to be a parent, but it's hard to do it well."

And, of course, we all want to be the best mom we can be. When Serena, an at-home mother of two boys, was experiencing morning sickness during her second pregnancy, she felt like she was too distracted to be a "good" mother to her first child. She says, "I'd made the choice to be home. I'd sacrificed something on the professional side of my life to be home with my kids, so I figured I better do it right. During the first trimester of my second pregnancy I felt horrible, so I didn't do much with my son because I felt so awful. I would feel so guilty. So there I was: sick as a dog and feeling guilty too. I kept thinking, 'Well, if I'm at home with my son, we should be doing more. I've only stimulated him once today.' I finally realized I was doing the best I could under the circumstances and that this situation wouldn't last forever."

How does the fact that a mother works affect her child? Elaine has a high-pressure job with a lot of travel. She loves her career but watches her two-year-old son for signs that he is negatively impacted by her work. She says, "I wonder if my working will really affect him. I was thinking about this on a business trip last week because I saw a mother and a small child walking together downtown. I thought that it would be great to walk down the street in the middle of the afternoon with my son. And I wondered, if I don't do those things will he be as happy a child or as fulfilled a person as if I did? In my heart, I really believe that's not the case. I observe him a lot to see if he's feeling needy, but he seems very secure. I'm proud that he seems okay regardless of my traveling. And I like to believe it's because of how my husband and I are raising him. He seems very sound and I hope that will be the case throughout his life whether I'm working or not."

Even being an at-home mom doesn't always quell our feelings of not being there "enough" for our children. Doreen, a mother of three who stays home, feels guilty that she isn't with her children more. She says, "I'm not working outside the home because my kids need me right now. I still struggle with the fact that I spend a certain amount of time away from my children every day. I have trouble with that. But on the other hand, I would get nothing done if I didn't do that. I'm chronically conflicted about that, but my kids seem to be happy and healthy and growing up just fine."

I Want to Work Differently

Whether we continue to work, stay at home, or do a combination of both, the important thing is to determine our priorities, then to live by them.

Necessity is the mother of invention. Or maybe mothers are necessarily inventive. In any case, one cannot help but be impressed with the creativity with which women have approached the work/family question. Since we are unable to work the way we did when we didn't have the responsibilities of motherhood, we must find new ways to work. Increasingly companies are instituting more family-friendly policies to help employees manage the work/family conflicts that arise. As mothers, we are changing our schedules through part-time work, flextime, compressed workweeks, and telecommuting from home to accommodate our families. Many of us have left corporate America to become independent contractors, work in smaller organizations, or start businesses of our own. In fact, the number of women-owned home-based businesses have increased ten-fold since 1980.[29] And some of us have left the workforce altogether and are using our professional skills in civic or volunteer work.

Many of us former career women who are now home with a baby or young children intend to go back to work later when our kids are older. Many of us, however, want to do something different than what we did in our pre-baby careers. A lot of stay-at-home mothers indicate that flexibility will be a key requirement of any future jobs. Many of us hope to work outside a corporate structure where we can have more control over our schedules and be free of big company politics. Many of us feel hopeful about the prospect of pursuing new professional interests when we return to the workforce.

Having children often helps us clarify our professional priorities. A consultant, Deborah was forty-one when her baby was born. She felt satisfied with her professional life and elected to cut back so she could focus on being a parent. She says, "I realized soon after my baby arrived that no matter how much I poured into my job, it was never going to be enough. My priorities became very clear. I liked my job. I needed my job, but I wasn't tying myself up in knots to meet their standards. So when I got an offer from another company, I started to see that my current work life was unacceptable. I took the offer and now am in a company where I don't have the management of people or the politics or pressure about hours. So I work the same number of hours, but they're much more rewarding and productive. And I feel that my son gives me an excuse. I can say 'no' to a lot of stuff that I would not have been strong enough to do without him."

Even if we don't do paid work, our job skills can benefit others — and ourselves. Rachael worked for eleven years before quitting to have a baby. She says she is very happy raising children and has no intention of going back to work if she doesn't have to. She plans to use her work skills in the volunteer sector. She says, "I really worked hard before I had kids and now I'm really happy to focus on them. I get a lot of fulfillment out of raising children. My daughter is a really nice kid, very kind and caring. I feel that my being around is making a difference with her. I'm doing volunteer work, so I feel like I'm helping other people and that's satisfying. I'm not bored and know that there are a lot of other things I want to do besides going back to work. I think I could be very happy not doing paid work ever again."

Sometimes staying at home with our children makes it possible for us to do work that we might not have done otherwise. Diane is writing a novel after many years in the financial field. She describes how being an author works well with being a mother: "Writing has always been an interest of mine, so now I'm combining something I like to do and the flexibility I need as a parent. It's important to me that I have a sense of doing something of my own, apart from my husband and apart from my children. I, like many women, have a diverse set of interests and didn't see myself doing the same job for my entire life anyway. To me, focusing on only one project is very limiting. I like pursuing an array of activities and am excited to be changing directions."

In a reversal of traditional roles, Sally is the primary breadwinner and her husband is at home with the children, ages three and one. She says, "When we got married, we envisioned that I might work part-time or work from home because my career was more flexible than my husband's. As time went on, it became clear that the long-term career path with my job was better from a flexibility and job satisfaction standpoint. We didn't think that I would be the one working and he would be the one staying home full-time, but it's worked out that way. As the parent who works, the hardest adjustment for me is that often my children will go to Daddy with a skinned knee or bumped head before they go to me. On the other hand, Mommy is kind of a special treat. My children are very well cared for, they're loved, and they seem secure. Mom works and Dad is home and they've never known it any other way."

The skills we practice as mothers can enhance our job skills. Lindsey left her job after she had her second child and plans to work again when her children are older. She says, "I've concluded that I'm becoming a better person because of my children and that, ultimately, being a mom will make me better on the job. With children, I'm improving my skills in organization, planning, delegation, and organizational behavior. I'm going to put 'Mother' on my resume when I go back to work. I don't want people to view this period as a gap but to know what I've been doing because I know it will make me a better employee. Some prospective employers may laugh, but others may stop and say, 'Hey, tell me about that.'"

As women who have had careers before becoming mothers, the decisions we make about work are complex and personal. Whether we continue to work, stay at home, or do a combination of both, the important thing is to determine our priorities, then to live by them. We are most happy when our decisions reflect our underlying values and when we can give our children the best of us without losing who we are. The more we talk to other new mothers about balancing work and family, the less we judge each other. We realize that we're all facing the struggle to find the right balance for our families and ourselves. And we must stay flexible because the balance we've struck today may not feel right down the road. Finally, we need to appreciate that, although it's not always easy, we're lucky we live in an era where we have so many choices about combining motherhood and work.

FOUR

Having a Baby Has Changed My Relationship with My Husband

Who of us is mature enough before the offspring themselves arrive? The value of marriage is not that adults produce children, but that children produce adults.

— *Peter De Vries*

The most important thing a father
can do for his children is to love
their mother.
— *Theodore Hesburgh*

While we're focusing on our own transition to parenthood, we often forget that our partners are undergoing a transition of their own. As women who have children at an older age, we are more set in our ways and are more certain about how our husbands *should* act as fathers. As part of a married couple without children, we had friends and interests independent of our husband, and significantly, time to pursue them. (Why didn't we appreciate that more then?) But when we become parents, our lives as a couple become more intertwined. At an emotional level, we are closer because of our shared love and responsibility for our child. And at a practical level, the logistics of running a family require the attention of two committed adults.

The irony is that having a baby can deepen our relationship with our husband while also pushing us apart. Tensions arise because women and men often view their parenting responsibilities differently and may have conflicting priorities and needs. It's upsetting when the normal stresses of having a baby make our relationship feel like a cause of strain rather than a source of comfort. Why can't our husband just read our minds and be sensitive to our every need? And we wonder whether we'll ever have a conversation with him again that isn't about scheduling logistics. Yet if we can join together and deal with the transition to parenthood as allies, we will find our relationship as a couple enriched and strengthened.

My Husband Is Afraid of Babies

Having grown up at a time when men were less active in child care, our husbands may not have learned how to nurture babies from their own fathers.

While we're trying to get the hang of motherhood, our husbands are embarking on the unfamiliar experience of becoming dads. Often it takes longer for a father to warm up to parenting, and many of our husbands are downright intimidated by newborns. Having grown up at a time when men were less active in child care, our husbands may not have learned how to nurture babies from their own fathers. In fact, Jay Belsky found in his study of couples becoming new parents that 70 percent of the men were slower than women in forming an attachment to the baby.[30]

A husband's discomfort with a new baby may reflect the ambivalence that many new parents feel toward the responsibility of being a parent. Samantha has three children and talks about her husband's behavior with babies: "At first, my husband had a hard time with the responsibility of being a parent.

This is someone who started his own business so it wasn't as if he was a stranger to responsibility. But there's no more 'in-your-face' responsibility than taking care of a new baby. He didn't like that stage. With our first baby, my husband was scared of being a dad and I was guilty of taking over too often. But he's been much better with the second and third children. He's much more comfortable and accepting of babies."

Luckily, ease with babies comes with experience. Joyce, an at-home mother of two, says: "I think that it took my husband a lot longer to make the transition to being a parent than it did me simply because being a parent was my full-time job and not his. That explains it as much as anything else. I'm the one logging the hours with our children. That's what makes me comfortable as a parent. Because my husband goes off to work every day, he doesn't have the same kind of time with them that I do. I have to keep reminding myself of that whenever I would find my expectations for him as a parent getting out of line."

Joyce comments on how her husband also has become more relaxed with their children as they get older: "What I've loved seeing is how my husband has become more and more comfortable with the kids. He was a little frightened of them when they were babies. That's not to say that he doesn't love them, but he doesn't really relate to them until they get to be about a year old. It's interesting because I think my husband feels that every time I have a child, he loses a part of me and I'm sure that's hard for him."

Being a Father Has Changed My Husband

We may be touched by the strength, vulnerability, and insight
they show as developing dads.

Although many of us feel that it's *our* lives that have been most impacted by having a baby, our husbands are also undergoing changes that alter their identity, behavior, and priorities. Whereas before we knew our partners as men and husbands, we view them in a different light now that they are fathers too. And though many new dads may not always live up to our ideal image of fatherhood, we may discover parts of their personalities that we didn't know existed. We may be touched by the strength, vulnerability, and insight they show as developing dads.

In becoming a father, some men may develop qualities that were undeveloped — or underdeveloped — before. Dana has a two-and-a-half-year-old daughter. She talks about how her husband has been impacted by having a baby: "I've really seen my husband soften. He's softening in a good way. He's learning how to get out of his own perspective, which is good. He's a very cerebral person and is very caught up in his mind. Sometimes it's hard for him to tune into our daughter. I've enjoyed seeing him starting to connect to her. It's been great to see him open up more."

Developing new characteristics and ways of dealing with

life can be hard. Stacey discusses the transition her husband and their relationship have undergone as they became parents: "My husband was a much more spontaneous soul before having a child. Now he has to plan his career, where we're going to live, and our lives. That's been a huge adjustment for him. We're past the adjustment, but it was painful and hard that first year. There was a time when there was a lot of resentment on his part for what he was missing. He was missing his sports and all the things he likes to do. His feelings struck me because I wasn't having those feelings, even though I wasn't doing all the things I used to do either. For me, being a parent of a small child is a phase. There will be a time when we can share our other interests with our daughter and that will be great. We've now been parents long enough that my husband has incorporated this new life into his old life. He's really taken to being a dad."

Seeing our husbands become responsible and caring fathers often deepens our respect for them. Valerie is most impressed with her husband's ability to create a caring relationship with their sons without models from his own childhood. She says, "I'm seeing sides of my husband that I haven't seen before. My greatest fear when we got married was that he had been raised in a very different family from mine and I didn't know what would happen when we started our own family. But he's a fantastic father and role model for our sons. It's wonderful for him to have sons because there's some healing going on there. I'm taking lessons from him, and my respect for him has grown on a daily basis. And even though we don't have the time together that we used to have, that respect has made our love deepen. Our love is growing in new ways because we have children."

Is This the Person I Married?

One of the confusing things about being parents is that we can feel both closer to and farther apart from each other.

The first several months of parenthood can be hard on our marriage because both members of the couple are trying to figure out how to be a family rather than two adults leading shared but separate lives. In Belsky's study, he observed that as new mothers and fathers we share our delight in the baby and have a fresh sense of ourselves as parents shaping the life of our child. However he also noted that new mothers and fathers have different concerns and needs. As women we expect our partners to help with the care of the baby and to be emotionally involved with the family. According to Belsky, new fathers need to feel financially secure and to continue to have some attention and affection from us as wives as well as some free time.[31]

Often conflict among couples with a new baby increases because issues that could be ignored before having a baby can no longer be overlooked. Much of the strain comes from our pre-baby expectations about the roles we would play as parents. As older mothers used to leading our own lives, we are learning to adapt to the responsibility of caring for a newborn and may resent the relative "freedom" that our husbands still enjoy. We can't believe that they can wake up on a Saturday morning and go out for a jog without even thinking about who will watch the baby. Yet our husbands are living with their own expectations and stresses. They are under pressure at work and feel that they need a "break" when they come home. And what happened to the woman they married? She's become obsessed by this tiny creature and no longer has time for him.

One of the confusing things about being parents is that we can feel both closer to and farther apart from each other. Leslie describes both the love she felt for her husband when they had a baby and the distance she felt from him during the first several months of her son's life: "I have a videotape of me in the hospital holding our baby, and I was overwhelmed with love and emotion (and probably Vicadin). I was filmed saying that this is the happiest day of my life, as happy as the other happiest day in my life when I married my husband. He was a great coach. I was so in love with him. I really wondered how couples could get divorced after creating a child together. It was incredible to me that he and I were now related to each other through this baby. I was so happy. It was everything I had hoped it would be."

Leslie's recollection continues, "Fast forward to six days later. I was having a terrible time breast-feeding. We were so convinced that breast-feeding was the only way to go — higher IQ, better SAT scores — this was important to us as a couple and it was not working. My son was losing weight. I was beside myself, and my husband went off to a sports event. He came home and I told him that I didn't really care if I ever saw him again. I felt that way for about seven months. I didn't really care too much about him because I had a baby that I loved so much. In retrospect, I realize it had a lot to do with my expectations. I wasn't the ideal mother, but I hadn't let go of my image of him as an ideal father. Now I have more realistic expectations about both of us and believe we'll be together forever."

The issue of our attention being focused on the baby to the exclusion of each other is a recurring one. Gina describes the transition she and her partner experienced after the birth of their son: "Having a baby created a lot of tension right away because my husband felt I was giving all my attention to the baby and not to him. It was very difficult for the first six months. I went back to work full-time after three months, so there was no time for us as a couple. He felt left out emotionally, and we had conflicts about how to raise the baby. I was in a constant state of exhaustion. I needed someone to cook me dinner and run a bath for me. My husband was feeling ignored most of the time. Slowly we got back on track because we do love each other very much. We got better at talking things out. When there was an argument, we wouldn't blow up. I started getting more sleep, which helped a lot, and he made an effort to be more understanding and supportive.

With time, we got back to a more balanced relationship."

Although most of us expect our partner to make a financial contribution to the family, his focus on his job during the baby years can cause friction in our relationship. While he perceives his increased commitment to work as providing financial security, we may view it as too much time away from the family. Barbara sums up the strains that occur now that her husband is the breadwinner and she is not working outside the home: She says, "The biggest adjustment for us as a couple is about money. We never argued over money before we had kids. I was used to earning money of my own and the truth is that money is power and a way of defining self-worth. Basically I'm getting a handout now, and I don't like being told what I can and cannot spend it on. But it's hard because my husband has no idea what it takes to run a household, so he can't imagine where the money is going. That's what causes a lot of our arguments now."

For most couples, clear communication decreases marital discord and disagreements. Cynthia and her husband parent differently. She has had to learn to express her needs and priorities more clearly since she became a mother. She says, "I remember being angry at my husband a lot after my first child was born. And what I learned is that he's not going to do anything the way I'm going to do it and it doesn't matter as long as the child is okay. I've also learned that I need to ask him for what I need and how I want it done. I'm very clear. So instead of getting angry because my expectations aren't met, I articulate them. If I have to go out to a meeting at night, I'll say to my husband that I want the kids to be in bed by the time I get back. They may not have brushed their teeth, but at least they're in bed when they should be. So instead of giving my husband a list of tasks, I just articulate the one most important thing and it gets done."

Without a doubt there is more pressure on our relationship when we have a child. The lesson for us as new mothers is that some disenchantment is normal especially in the initial stages of parenthood. It takes time for our partnership to expand to include our new roles as parents. With time we find ways to communicate better with our husbands, set mutual priorities, and manage our disagreements in a way that is satisfying to both of us.

We Argue More Than We Used To

In his study, Belsky observed that the reason the division of household chores creates so much discord is that the work required to care of a home and a new baby does increase significantly.

Many arguments during the postpartum period center on who will do the work associated with a new baby and who will make the sacrifices in their career that having a family entails. Before having a baby, many of us thought of our marriage as a relationship between equals. As such, we expected our partner's contribution to parenting to be similar to ours. Yet when we have a baby, we are surprised by the traditional roles we find ourselves playing. When it comes down to it, the great majority of mothers, including working mothers, still have primary responsibility for managing the home and family, while Dad focuses on being the money maker. It's Mom who buys the diapers, coordinates the child care, and makes sure the baby has her regular checkups. And because of these child-care responsibilities, we are the ones who make concessions in our careers. Although some of us do so willingly, others of us resent the fact that we have to scale back our professional lives — which of course we take out on our spouses.

In his study, Belsky observed that the reason the division of household chores creates so much discord is that the work required to care of a home and a new baby does increase significantly. On average, a couple without children did one load of laundry a week, prepared meals twice a day, and cleaned house once a week. A family with a new baby does four to five loads of laundry a week, prepares four meals a day, and cleans house once a day.[32] This is in addition to caring for the baby. No wonder the division of labor becomes such a big issue.

Some of the stress comes from the norms and expectations we bring to parenthood. While we may compare our husbands to ourselves and feel that they're not doing as much of the child care as we are, they may be comparing themselves to their fathers and feel that they're doing a lot. And while we're trying to balance our own careers and interests with having a family, even our enlightened husbands may have expectations for us that are based on women in their mothers' generation, the majority of whom focused on children and home above all else.

How to divide the work of caring for a baby and a home is an issue for most new parents. Amy articulates the dynamic: "When we had a baby, things that hadn't been issues became issues. For instance, I work full-time and was doing 80 percent of the household responsibilities. I had been for years, but it hadn't been a big deal. When we had the baby, I started to crack. I was resentful of the time I spent doing those things because I wanted to spend that time with my daughter."

Problems may also arise when an at-home mother wants a reprieve from the demands of child rearing. Joanne, the mother of two sons, says, "I'm home full-time with my kids, so I'm more comfortable with the unrelenting action and activities. The conflicts I have with my husband come on the weekends when we're both home, both want a break, and more often than not the kids come to me with their needs. I'm not able to relax. This is getting better as I've been able to tell my husband how I feel and how he can take some of the burden off me."

If we share many of the parenting responsibilities, we may also have to relinquish some of our authority over family matters. Teresa says, "I think because I was the one on maternity leave, I got in the pattern of doing all the child-related jobs. I ended up taking more responsibility by default. Even after I went back to work, I was in a pattern of taking care of all those things, and I had to stop and ask myself, 'Where's the balance?' But I've accepted my responsibility for wanting it this way. I want to be the one who knows certain things and runs things a certain way. And I've discovered that when I have to travel for business and my husband is in charge, the program changes. I have to respect that and respect that my husband has been on duty full-time. I'm lucky because my husband wants to be involved, but it's a tug-of-war sometimes."

Adjusting our professional life to accommodate our home life is an ongoing process. At age thirty-five, Rebecca is pregnant with her second child. At times, there has been stress in her marriage over the concessions that she's made in her career. She says, "I have a full-time job, and although there have been difficult times, we have a great day-care situation so we've been able to make it work. It's going to be a lot more expensive to have two children in day care, and my husband is going to be traveling more for his job. I already see that I'm the one who is going to have to make adjustments to be around home more. I resent that, but I don't see how we can do it any other way. I believe it will all work out if we can just stay focused on the priorities."

Resentment can grow when we feel we are more tied down by the baby than our husbands. Jocelyn says, "I remember my husband saying before the baby was born that a baby didn't need to change your life. Now he admits that having a baby is a lot of work. On the other hand, last weekend he went out to play basketball with his friends. I was furious. I didn't quite understand why and then I realized it was because he *could* just go out. I could never do that. I wouldn't even think of doing that. And to think he could actually do that without even saying, 'Would you like to go out and I'll stay here and look after the baby?' I realized that sometimes I needed to say to him, 'I need my time off too.'"

Jocelyn continues to discuss how different her expectations of sharing the parental duties are from the reality: "It's funny, I went through my life as an adult thinking I was leading a more progressive life than my parents. And now here I am — the wife at home waiting with the baby for the husband to get home from work! All of a sudden I've become a housewife who is nagging her husband to pick his clothes up off the floor. I never expected that."

My Husband Feels Left Out

We use up our patience on our child and then don't have much left for our husband.

With so much of our attention focused on the new baby, our husband often feels left out. There are not enough hours in the day for us to care for a baby, do our work (paid or unpaid), and spend quality time with our husbands. We end up concentrating our limited time and energy on the baby.

While many of us believe in the importance of having a strong marriage, attending to our husband can seem like "just one more thing to do," especially in the first six months when we are totally absorbed with our new baby. Jill says, "The one thing I feel guilty about is that I put my daughter first, before my husband. Luckily he's pretty laid back, and over the last several years, I've put a lot of time and effort into our relationship, so hopefully he doesn't feel too bad. I noticed a change when our daughter was around six months old. My husband and I have started becoming closer again. I felt like I could take some of my attention away from my daughter and focus on him. I wanted to. It's partly because my husband can take care of himself whereas the baby can't. And it's partly because having a child has been the most wonderful thing I've ever done, and I want to savor the whole experience."

When we have children, we aren't as easygoing as we used to be because we don't have as much capacity to be flexible. We use up our patience on our child and then don't have much left for our husband. As Dana puts it, "As far as our relationship goes, I've found that if I've allotted a certain amount of patience in the day, I'll devote 90 percent of it to my daughter and only have 10 percent left for my husband. When I've had to choose between taking care of my daughter's needs and taking care of my husband's needs, I've chosen my daughter's. Sometimes I feel that my husband suffers undeservedly."

Although easy to forget when consumed by a new baby,

it's important for us to consciously remember how important our husbands are. Caroline has four children and talks about the role her husband plays in their life as a family: "My husband is my biggest source of support. Everything in our family life starts at home. I think that a lot of mothers make a big mistake forgetting that their husband is half of the marriage and half of the parents. But you have to remember that there's someone else important in the life of your children, and that's their father. That's not to say I always act that way myself. When the babies were little, I ignored my husband. Essentially I said to him, 'Sorry, honey, I can't talk now, I'm trying to keep a baby alive.' But now I realize that my relationship with my husband is the foundation of our family life."

Having Kids Has Strengthened Our Relationship

New baby tensions in our marriage often force us to work through our conflicts.

Many of us feel that having children has enriched our marriage and given it more meaning. With our husband, we are pursuing the mutual goal of creating a happy family. Despite moments of disenchantment with our spouse, raising children together can solidify our relationship. As a family, we become part of something bigger and more important. And having children creates opportunities for couples to experience more fulfillment, disappointment, and ultimately growth.

A baby often has a positive impact on our relationship with our husbands. Heather, the mother of a three-month-old, says, "It's made us closer than ever. We share something that we don't share with anyone else in the world. Even though we said vows to each other when we got married, it wasn't really until we had a child that we felt like we were in this forever. My husband sees me taking care of the baby and he's much more attentive to my needs. He's less selfish. He doesn't always take care of the baby in the same way I do, but I know the baby is safe with him. My husband has incredible patience and relates to children really well. He hasn't done as much of the initial caretaking as I have, but I don't worry about it because I know he'll be very involved as our baby gets older, maybe more so than I will be."

New baby tensions in our marriage often force us to work through our conflicts. Bonnie says, "My relationship with my husband is totally different now that we're parents. We're no longer a couple. We're a mother and father, and that's changed how we interact with each other. We knew each other well before we got married. First we were very good friends. Then we got married. We went through a loss together. We bought a house together. We did all those stressful things that build a relationship. Sometimes there are things that we're having problems with as individuals that come up with our child and it drives me mad. But we're lucky because we can talk about these things. I have a husband who works at our marriage. I sometimes think we're about to get a divorce because we approach things so differently and the thought never occurs to him. As parents, we're in this for the long haul."

Having kids can strengthen our relationships as couples when we learn to communicate more directly with one another. Doreen, a mother of three, says, "We go through waves of making adjustments in our relationship. We used to be able to communicate through telepathy. Now that we have kids we've had to really work at saying what we want. The first year was very difficult, but we got past that and have learned to be more verbal about our needs. It's been a learning process. The times when I felt he didn't understand where I was were really hard, but when we could finally address it, the relationship was strengthened. And so much of it is that with children you are facing your most fundamental issues, fears, and values. We want to consciously raise our children instead of just going through the motions, so we have to be on the same wavelength."

Will We Ever Have Sex Again?

"One of the most challenging aspects of parenting is finding energy for your own relationship — both sexual and emotional.

It's amazing how little interest most of us have in sex after having a baby. While our husbands are eager to resume a physical relationship, our preoccupation with motherhood makes it difficult to focus on anything else. Fundamentally we have a hard time envisioning ourselves as sexual creatures. In our minds there are a hundred reasons not to have sex, which is in direct contrast to the hundred reasons our husbands think we should. We're exhausted. We're nursing. We're ten pounds overweight. We've held our baby all day long and don't want to be touched. A study by the University of Michigan confirms that the incidence of sexual intercourse between couples drops 30 to 40 percent in the first year of parenthood.[33] Despite our reasons to the contrary, being physically intimate with our husbands can help re-create some of the emotional intimacy that may be missing from our lives as a couple with a brand-new baby.

Gina describes the evolution in her romantic relationship. For the first nine months after having a baby she was exhausted, but as she started to get more sleep, she felt she could give her husband more attention. She says, "At nine months, we started to go out again. I finally figured out that I needed to do things to let him know that I was thinking about him. It didn't have to be a lot: buy him flowers every once in a while, get a baby-sitter, have sex. Concentrating on him made a huge difference. When he was feeling cared about, he was more supportive of me. It took me a while to figure that out, but eventually it's worked itself out."

Adoption can also affect our sexual relationship. Melissa, the mother of an adopted baby, reports that her sex life with her husband was curtailed when their baby arrived. She says, "I didn't even give birth and our sex life changed dramatically. It's just that our lives are so different as parents, we don't have the time or energy for sex."

Sheer fatigue plays a big role in diminished intimacy. Joanne describes the difficulty in finding the energy to maintain a romantic relationship while caring for small children: "One of the most challenging aspects of parenting is finding energy for your own relationship — both sexual and emotional. I'd say it comes in waves. A lot of time can pass without having time for intimacy, and tensions build. When we do find time, we're closer. I never doubt our love for one another, but it's a lot of juggling. Especially for at-home moms, trying to make that leap into being a sexual person in the same room where you've been changing diapers, nursing, and breaking up fights is difficult!"

Many new mothers experience a range of feelings about their husbands as fathers. Elise says, "I feel like I'm missing some of the romance from our relationship and it makes me crazy. Does it mean that I should be looking for something else if I don't always feel romantic toward my husband? I love my husband and feel like we're connected as a family unit. I feel this great bond. My husband, daughter, and I do group hugs, where we all kiss each other. It's really cute, but then I think, 'Is this a substitute for romance?' We have sex but not as much as he would like. But I don't miss it that much. Then I think, what's wrong with me, should I be wanting more? Is this a sign that I shouldn't be married to this man even though I can't imagine life without him? And yet I love our whole family unit, it's so beautiful to me."

One of the mysteries of mothering is how wonderful it is to share a child with your husband despite the fact that your relationship will never be the same as when you were just a couple. Sandra, the mother of a two-year-old, says, "It's difficult to lose the romantic intimacy of the years when my husband and I were just a couple. But I see so much of my husband in my daughter and when I catch his expressions in her eyes or see his face in her face, I am consumed with a wild love for her and for him and for him in her. It's the most incredible feeling I've ever had to see the person I love the most in the other person I love the most."

We Feel Closer When We Make Time for Each Other

Each couple needs to find its own way to keep the romance alive.

Most of us know what a gift it is to our children to have a good marriage, yet it's difficult to make our relationship a priority among so many urgent priorities when we're new parents. It takes some effort to have a "date" with our partner, yet it's important to spend time with our husband to remind ourselves how much we really do like this person who fathered our child. A "date" for new parents can be as simple as dinner and a movie (if we can both stay awake that late) or as luxurious as a weekend away. The important thing is for us to create time outside of our routine to focus on our romantic relationship.

Each couple needs to find its own way to keep the romance alive. Janine, who has a two-year-old, says, "We have a regular baby-sitter once a week, which forces us to go out without the baby. Sometimes the baby-sitter arrives and all I want to do is go to bed, but since she's there, we go. It's helped our relationship to be together as adults every now and then, not just as parents. Without regularly checking in, we end up going in two different directions for too long and that's not good for our relationship."

MaryAnne, a mother of two daughters, says, "For me it's all an issue of balance. My husband and I don't have a regular date night because it doesn't fit into our schedules. However, I find that when things are getting off-kilter, we do need to spend some time together and just have fun. Time away from our children and time to ourselves gives us back some sense of control in our lives and our relationship."

Even though it was scary to leave her newborn, Caroline has hired baby-sitters since each of her children were two months old so she could go out with her husband. She says, "It was hard but I felt it was important to have 'dates' with Daddy right from the beginning. I want my children to know that Dad is an important person in Mom's life. I want them to see me taking a bath, putting on perfume, and wearing my hot jeans for their father. I believe that their seeing us having fun together makes them feel happy and secure."

We'll Still Be Together When the Kids Are Gone

Sometimes just listening to each other is what we need most.

In another study of new parents, Cowan and Cowan found that it's helpful to focus on what unites us as parents rather than the issues that force us apart.[34] This is not to say that conflicts should be ignored. As men and women, our differences in needs, priorities, and values will arise, and we need to reconcile them. But sometimes we also need to focus on our relationship as a couple. As new mothers and fathers, we will redefine our relationship and expectations throughout the course of parenthood. Having some empathy for our partner and working through the transition together can improve our relationship and create mutual respect.

Sometimes just listening to each other is what we need most. By each having a turn to speak and be heard, Janet and her husband are making an emotional investment in each other and their relationship. She says, "A lot of people talk about how they keep the romance alive, but what I try to do is maintain a connection. It's hard when you haven't seen each other, you've both had a long day, and you're tired. So what we do is these listening partnerships. It's important to do at the end of the day after the kids are in bed. We each get five minutes and we take turns talking without being interrupted by the other person. Then we switch. It's so great because I get to really hear what's up with him: what's exciting or hard. It's not about responding or validating. When it's my turn, I get a chance, without problem solving, to just say what's up for me. Sometime it can be ugly, but these are the things we want each other to know. After I've been heard, the pressure lifts off me. When I do this on a regular basis, I feel connected with my husband and what's going on in his life."

Expressing appreciation helps keep a marriage alive. Denny and her husband, the parents of a two-year-old, try to show their appreciation for one another by keeping a gratitude journal: "We write in it daily," she says. "We recap the day and try to come up with three things for which we are grateful. They can be big things or small things, such as 'thanks for giving the baby a bath.' Then we exchange journals with each other. It changes the way you look at your partner and keeps you thinking positively about your life. You don't get bogged down so much by the daily grind. If we don't have time to write, then we just tell each other what we appreciate about each other. It's a nice way to end the day because it only takes a few minutes and makes you feel closer."

A mother of two, Eve talks about the importance of showing compassion for each other and keeping things in perspective. She says, "Having small children is a very challenging period in a relationship. It's a very intense time when your children are at their most needy, and professionally, you or your spouse is hoping to crest. You're working toward your professional objectives, yet there are so many other demands and expectations at home. It's not a restful, easy time. But if you can just get through it and enjoy each other, even if you don't have as much of each other as you want, that can be really helpful. I try to remember that at some point in the future, we'll have more time and energy for each other. It's not always going to be this way."

Despite the "wear and tear" that children have on a marriage, studies show that most parents are thrilled to have children and would make the same decision all over again.[35] Cowan and Cowan's studies show us that even though conflicts and disagreements are inevitable following the birth of a baby, they are a normal part of becoming a new family. Those couples that can successfully make the shift to parenthood will develop new insights and new ways to solve problems, in addition to experiencing a greater sense of maturity.[36] Our development as a couple comes through the ongoing process of listening to each other and successfully resolving the issues that having children presents. If we can focus on the shared joy of parenting and face the trials and tribulations with humor, we will grow as individuals and as partners. And as we grow as a couple, we improve our ability to raise our children.

FIVE

How Will Our Parents Be Involved with Our New Family?

Every time a child is born, a grandparent is born too. Parents cannot choose to be grandparents any more than children can choose to be born.

— *Arthur Kornhaber*

The simplest toy, one which even the youngest child can operate, is called a grandparent.
— Sam Levenson

Many of us who worked and established careers out of college have led lives that are quite different from the ones our mothers led. Whereas the norm for us is to pursue a career before having a family, our mothers generally had babies at a younger age and, most likely, did not establish themselves in a profession in their young adulthood. But having a baby gives us something in common with our mother and makes us appreciate her more. Our parents, in turn, may have new respect for us as adults and parents. Through our baby, we share an identity as parents as well as our love for the same incredible person — our child! And our parents can be an enormous source of support, especially when we have a newborn (and we're willing to take advice from anyone — even our own mothers).

At the same time, having a baby can present new opportunities for tension with our parents and in-laws. Disagreements may arise over our values, parenting styles, and even visiting rights. Our relationship may change since we are no longer "the kids," and our parents are no longer "in charge." We may have different expectations than our parents about the role they will play and the level of involvement they will have with our family. Yet most of us want our children to know and love their grandparents. The differences among generations can be worked out with patience, flexibility, and open dialogue so we can enjoy the benefits of an extended family.

We're Closer to Our Parents Now That We Have Kids

A baby can help us open up to our parents in new ways.

Having children often makes us closer to our own parents as our relationship with them takes on a new dimension. Part of it is that the bond between child and grandparent is second only to the bond between child and parent. Our parents experience the delight of spending time with our baby, without the complications of being the primary caretaker or rule setter. Or in other words, they have all the fun, then get to go home. In addition, having a child diffuses some of the emotional intensity of our relationship with our parents. The focus shifts more to the baby and less on the aspects of our relationship that create discord between us. And by spending more time with our parents around small children, we learn more about them as they relive their own experience of raising a family.

One of the pleasures of having children is that we may become closer to our own parents. Judy was thirty-nine when she had her son, who is now four months old. She says, "Having a baby has definitely brought me closer to my own nts. They spend a lot of time with us. My mother has .eally taken to being a grandmother. It's meant a lot to my parents for us to have a baby because we waited so long. They're getting older and their health is starting to fail. So I'm much more conscious of their being involved with my son's birth, growth, and development. It's a very emotional time for me because I'm starting to see the decline of the family I grew up in. I really want my parents to be a part of my son's life and our life as a family."

In some cases, even difficult relationships with parents can become easier when we have children. Elaine describes how her relationship with each of her parents has improved since the birth of her son, who is now two years old. She says, "I don't have the greatest relationship with my mother, but our baby has drawn my mother and me closer. We have a common joy. I see the delight he brings her and it makes me happy because she hasn't had the easiest life. I love seeing the smile on her face when she's with him. With my dad, having a baby has made him think of me as an adult. He's incredulous that his little girl is a mother. He's also been a lot of help and provided me with a support system. Being a grandfather has meant a lot to him."

A baby can help us open up to our parents in new ways. Samantha, a mother of three, says, "I'm much closer to my parents. I was always close to them, but I was always a pretty private person. Before, I would report to them on school, my job, my friends, but now we have this common bond and project. They are infatuated with my children. They're interested in everything they do and are very emotionally invested in them. My parents aren't the types that drop in for an hour then leave. They want to wash the car with my kids and feed the dog and rake the leaves. They don't want to do only special things. They really like the common daily tasks, because they feel that that's how you get to know each other."

I Still Need My Parents

*As older mothers who are used to being on our own, we may
be surprised by how much we still rely on Mom and Dad.*

As we become parents and embark on one of the most emotionally and physically powerful experiences of our lives, to whom do we turn? Often it's our own mothers and fathers. Despite our imperfect relationships, our parents are always our parents, especially when we are at our most vulnerable. As older mothers who are used to being on our own, we may be surprised by how much we still rely on Mom and Dad. And it may be awkward for us to ask for their help after so many years of being self-sufficient. Yet our parents can be a tremendous source of emotional support and practical advice, if we allow them to be. Often they are eager to come help us with our new baby and take care of us. And as parents ourselves, we no longer take their love for and commitment to us for granted.

When we have a baby, we appreciate our parents in new ways. Ann Marie, age thirty-five, says that having a baby made her realize how important her mother is to her. She says, "I still need my mother. No one else is going to be there in quite the same way. I feel like she's the only person that would get on a plane and come if I said I needed her. And when she comes, she's doing it for me. She's here to take care of me. Who else would do that?"

But sometimes having a child can cause strain as well. Ann Marie continues, "I have great parents, but the moment my baby was born, our relationship shifted back a little more to a parent/child dynamic. I had been on my own for a long time before having a child. I lived in a different city, and I had been financially independent for a while. I'd pretty much done what I wanted to do without consulting them. But the minute I had the baby, my mom started giving me advice again. The last person you want advice from is your mother or mother-in-law. I didn't want them to tell me how to parent at all. But I find that my mother always has something useful to offer. I fight it, but usually end up doing what she says."

Our parents give the gift of themselves, which enriches our children's lives. LeeAnn feels fortunate that her parents are so involved in her two-year-old daughter's life and sees how much her mother has benefited from spending time with the baby. She says, "My mom baby-sits for us one day a week and has since our daughter was born. She's an enormous help, and I think it's so wonderful that she and my little girl have that regular time together. My daughter's completely comfortable with my mom, and I'm much more relaxed than I am when my daughter is with our baby-sitter because I know she's in such good hands. There's someone who cares as much for her as I do who's looking out for her. My mother was quite sick before our baby was born, and I see how being with her granddaughter has given her a new lease on life. I know that my parents enhance my daughter's life by bringing parts of themselves that my husband and I don't have. I hope they live long lives and help shape who she is."

But we can't count on a difficult relationship with our parents getting better just because we have children. Sharon has not been close to her parents since she was a young adult, talks about how having a baby has opened up old wounds. She wishes her parents would take more of an interest in her daughter. She says, "Having a baby has impacted my psychological relationship with my parents but not my day-to-day relationship. I'm not close to my parents anyway, but it's been hard for me that they haven't been very interested in the baby. She's not getting the attention and emotional involvement from them that I'd like her to have. I had accepted that they aren't good parents to me, but reexperiencing it is painful. I'm sorry that they can't be more interested, because they're the ones missing out. I'm glad for our daughter that my husband's parents are such loving grandparents."

Stepparents can play an important role in our lives and in our children's lives. Antonia talks about the support she gets from her stepmother for being a mother: "Whenever we are with my stepmom, she is unbelievably supportive of how I am doing as a mom. One thing I want to do as well as my stepmom does is to give my kids that sense that I am on their side and think they are the best no matter what. My stepmother always takes my side, which I really treasure."

I Expect My Parents to Play a Different Role Than They Do

In addition to serving as nurturers, role models, playmates, and keepers of the family flame, grandparents can provide a place where our children know they will be appreciated and accepted.

When our parents become grandparents, they take on a new role within the family. Like it or not, they become part of the older generation. And just as parental roles today are changing, so are those for grandparents. We may be parenting differently than our mothers and fathers did, and they may not understand our style of mothering or lifestyle choices. For instance, our parents may not appreciate the role work plays in our life and the struggles we face to balance a job and a family. Or they may not be used to fathers participating in child care. Or with so many of our parents becoming grandparents while they're still active, they may have less interest in baby-sitting than in pursuing their own interests. We may ease some of the tension, however, if we think more flexibly about the role a grandparent plays in our family. In addition to serving as nurturers, role models, playmates, and keepers of the family flame, grandparents can provide a place where our children know they will be appreciated and accepted.

Some parents, like Marion's, really take to being grandparents. She says, "Now that we have kids, my parents are around all the time. Luckily my husband has a very easy relationship with them, and they're very respectful of how we're raising our family. My mother went very smoothly from the role of mother to the role of grandmother. She didn't need to be the center of the family. I don't think she was comfortable with that role in the first place. She's the one that spoils my kids. And my dad's role is to be their playmate. He gets down on the floor with them and plays all their silly games. They call him by his first name and tell him he can't play with their toys. My children love both of them."

Our parents may have mixed feelings about becoming grandparents. Although they like the idea of having a baby in the family, they may have to get over their own prejudices about what being a grandparent entails. Grace says, "My mother took a while to warm up to the notion of being a grandmother. She was in her late fifties, and I think the whole idea made her feel like she was getting old. But once she realized that it was inevitable that she was going to be a grandmother, she really embraced the role. Now she goes around showing the kids' photos and telling stories about them to any-one who will listen. I think she's come to the conclusion that she doesn't have to be like her grandmother, who was one of those little old ladies in print dresses and orthopedic shoes."

Just as we sometimes have to rework our expectations of ourselves as parents, we may also need to adjust our expecta-tions of our parents as grandparents. Eve has two children and is pregnant with her third baby. She talks about her parents not living up to her expectations and how she's had to rethink her assumptions about them. She says, "I love my parents dearly, but my mother is not a 'hands-on' baby person, which I just should have acknowledged from the beginning. Instead I had unbelievably artificial expectations for her that were not met. She tried to meet them with the second baby. She came and stayed when the baby was born, and it was a huge mis-take. But she and my father have been great grandparents as my kids have gotten older. I just needed to adjust my expec-tations to what they're really like and good at and not demand that they be different."

Teresa speaks warmly of her parents but observes that the nature of her relationship with them has changed because her son has become the focus of their attention. She says, "My parents are very respectful of our space. My mom went back to a second career, so I feel like I'm trying to get her time. She does things like taking my son to work with her. It's weird in some ways, because I don't feel like I have as much access to my parents as 'me' anymore. I don't have them in the same way. Their focus is on my son. I'm just the host so I can deliver the perfect child to my parents, so they can take him to church and show him off to their friends."

I Now Have My Parents' Approval

Although proud of us for graduating from college, doing well at a job, and being financially independent, many of our parents really want us to start a family.

Some of us feel that becoming a mother earned our parents' approval in a way that our other "accomplishments" never quite did. Although proud of us for graduating from college, doing well at a job, and being financially independent, many of our parents *really* want us to start a family. This may feel strange to us, especially if they always encouraged us to pursue an education and a career. For grandparents, a new baby in the family can bring pleasure, a sense of being needed, and a promise of living into the future. And as a new mother, we are playing a role our parents understand and support, in part because they know the fulfillment they experienced raising young children of their own.

Gaining our parents' approval when we have a baby doesn't necessarily mean that they don't approve of other aspects of our life, although sometimes it may feel that way. Wendy says, "Having a baby was much more of a big deal for my parents than anything else I'd done. It was bigger than going to graduate school or getting married. I got a lot of approval for being a mother, even though they were also very encouraging of my going to back to work and not sacrificing all that I'd done in my job. But they were *really* happy when we had a baby."

Pregnant with her second child, Rebecca says that now that she has a family, she's living up to her mother's expectations in a way she wasn't when she was a career woman. She relates, "Now that I have a baby, I'm at a point with my mother where I'm living up to her expectations. When I was single, I really wasn't. Now I'm married to a man she loves and I have a baby. It's too bad that I had to do all these things to gain her approval, but it's brought us together."

Our parents may feel their own confusion about balancing work and family, which of course they pass on in some form to us. Teresa laughs about the fact that her mother was very supportive of her having a career and yet seems most impressed that she had a baby. She says, "In some ways, I gained my mother's approval when I had a baby because I gave her something she really wanted. The biggest irony of my life as a professional working mom is that my mom was at home. It's because of her that I'm who I am. She had confidence in me and made me believe I could do anything I wanted. She was disciplining me and enforcing values and helping me be who I am. She raised me to be a career woman and hire someone to take care of my kids, as opposed to what she did, which was to stay home. When I get stressed about work, my mom will say, 'Sweetie, why are you worried? You have your baby. That's your reward.' It's as if my professional aspirations were temporary, and being a mother was my true calling. It's funny because it's such an unliberated view from a mother who wanted her daughter to be able to do anything she put her mind to."

I Really Miss My Family

When we have children, the realities of our mobile society may hit us in ways that they haven't before.

Many of us moved away from home as young adults and now live apart from our parents. Although we missed them before, now that we have children, we really feel the distance. We wish our parents lived closer for our children's sake as well as our own. We long for their involvement in our children's lives and regret that they aren't around to provide us practical and emotional support. We find that we need to make more of an effort for our children to get to know their grandparents (and vice versa) when they live so far away. Yet we're willing to make that effort, because we want our children to have an intimate relationship with their grandparents.

When we have children, the realities of our mobile society may hit us in ways that they haven't before. Julia, for instance, questions the distance among her family members. She says, "In terms of my present life there's a great joy in sharing my children with my parents. It's made me wish we lived closer together. It's made me question why communities don't stay together. Why don't we raise our children near our parents so we can all be more involved in each other's lives day-to-day? Because when they're this age, children are so much about the day-to-day. I wish my parents could be more a part of this."

The working mother of a two-year old, Elise expresses her disappointment that her parents have moved recently: "I'm frustrated with my family right now because they moved so far away. In my own selfish way, I'm angry with them that they left the area. I want them to be around to have a relationship with my daughter, and I would really love it if they were around to help me."

Depending on how well we get along with our parents, some of us believe that living far away is not such a bad thing. Living apart allows us to maintain a comfortable distance from our parents. Wendy says, "It's not totally by chance that I live in a different part of the country than my parents. I love them, but they really do drive me crazy. If they lived near us, they would be so overinvolved with my family that it's worked out well that they live farther away. This way they come visit us a few times a year and we all enjoy each other. If they were around more, I think we'd drive each other nuts."

I Feel Like I'm the Adult Now

As parents, we experience a new equality with our parents.

When our baby is born and we become parents, we often feel that we have finally grown up. This puts us on a different level with our parents who have always been the responsible adults in the family. Many of us feel that although we rely on our parents for help and support, we're no longer dependent on them. By having a baby, our mothers and fathers become members of the next generation, and the authority and attention shifts to us as new parents. We feel that our new families begin to take center stage, and that we need to start establishing our own priorities, values, and traditions.

Sharing the experience of motherhood can strengthen our relationship with our mothers. Cynthia says, "As I get older, I have more like experiences with my mother so our relationship is deeper. I'm not a child anymore. I am her child, and I am also her friend. I've been her friend a long time, but now I'm more of a peer, because we share the motherhood experience. She doesn't give me advice unless I ask for it. She doesn't look over my shoulder and tell me if I'm doing something wrong, and she never has. That's probably why I have such a good relationship with her as a mother. She's always treated me with respect, and I've always respected her."

Putting old family problems to rest allows us to focus on

our children's needs. Stacey, the mother of a two-year-old, says, "If there is any negative in my relationship with my parents, it's with regard to their divorce. That has to be behind all of us now. I don't want their unfinished business to affect our holidays or family events. I'm very oriented toward my daughter and her future. I'm done with the past and with my parents' problems. I'm not sure that they're completely done with their past, and to the extent that I have to consider that, it seems wrong. We all have to move on because the time now is for this young child."

As parents, we experience a new equality with our parents. Joyce, a mother of two, describes how having children has made her relate to her mother as more of a peer: "I'm not really my mother's child anymore. I will always be her daughter, but I'm no longer her child. I'm her daughter, but I have my own family now. Things have changed. My mother went through some transition pains in that respect, realizing that I had my own family and that my family was my priority. She couldn't be the priority anymore. And I think I went through a transition too. It took me a number of years to come to grips with that. We're more on par as adults and that's how it should be."

I Have New Insight into My Mother

We begin to understand the powerful love our mothers felt for us and the struggles they faced to raise a family.

Many of us have new appreciation and compassion for our parents, especially our mothers, after becoming mothers ourselves. We begin to understand the powerful love our mothers felt for us and the struggles they faced to raise a family. We empathize with the commitment and sacrifices they made. When we become mothers, we feel a common identity with our mothers and can begin to view them as human beings with both strengths and flaws. At the same time, our mothers may benefit from having grandchildren because they can have relationships with our children that they may have been unable to have with us. Becoming a grandparent can give them a second chance to be more emotionally available and nurturing then they were as a parent in the 1950s and 1960s.

Becoming parents gives us a new perspective on our own parents. Pam says, "I am more appreciative of my own parents now that I have children. I've learned a lot from them and have a lot more respect for them. I realize now that they did a really good job with me and my brothers, and I hope to do as good a job with my kids."

Not only do we grow and change when we have a child, so do our parents. Marcia, a single mother of a two-year-old, describes her relationship with her parents. She says, "I spend a lot more time with my parents now that I'm a mother. They were instrumental in my baby's care the first year. It's really been interesting to watch my mother with my daughter, because I think she's trying to make up with her what she didn't do with us. In her day, when a child started to walk, you noticed it but didn't get excited. It was part of the routine. With my daughter, with every single milestone, she's more excited than I am. It's opened her up a lot emotionally to have my daughter around. It's made us closer."

Marcia goes on, "I know my mom was a pretty good parent because I turned out okay. I'm a good parent, because she was a good parent to my siblings and me. But our generation has opened up new wells of emotions that the prior generation didn't acknowledge. We have a combination of their basic values and good parenting, and we get to refine it by being more loving and physical with our kids."

Now that we have our own family, we may have more empathy for our mothers even when we approach motherhood with a different set of objectives. Audrey says, "My expectation of my relationship with my child is totally different than what my mother expected of herself emotionally. I expect a relationship and put a lot of energy into it. My mother had six children, so motherhood was more of an organizational feat. I remember telling my mother how much I loved my son when he was a baby. I asked my mother if she felt the same way. I respect my mom for her honesty, but she said she didn't think so. That wasn't what it was about. You grew up, got married, had kids, and did your best not to go nuts. And her job was to manage us all, not to relate to us. That's why I can count on one hand the times I spent with her. So I think we're trying to achieve very different things than our mothers were trying to achieve. Had she been trying to do what I'm trying to do, it would have made her crazy."

As we experience motherhood, we may begin to understand our own mother's experience more fully. Heather says she now has appreciation for the fulfillment her mother felt raising children: "Having a baby has given me a better understanding of my mother. After she had children, she never worked again. I always thought that she had shortchanged herself. But now I see that raising kids is a difficult path to choose and that she did a good job. I can see now that she could feel a lot of satisfaction in that. I realize how she could reconcile her own life and be very happy being a mother."

It's Hard Being a Mom without My Mother

We may miss our mother because there are so many questions we'd like to ask her.

Becoming a mother can be bittersweet for those of us who have lost our own mothers. We miss them and feel sad that our mothers and our babies will never know each other. We feel cheated because we can't turn to our mothers for help or advice. And they aren't around to tell us stories and give us perspective about the early years of our lives. We wish our mother could see us as a mom, because we know she would be proud of us. Having a baby can make us feel the continuity of life and the connection between our mother and the future. And as we experience maternal love ourselves, we may compensate, in part, for the absence of it in our own lives.

We may miss our mother because there are so many questions we'd like to ask her. Nicole, who has two sons, says, "I miss my mother because there's no one around that I can go to for practical advice. Sometimes when I'm sewing a Halloween costume or baking holiday cookies I think, 'Where is my mother?' These are the things she was so good at and as a grandmother she would have a lot more time to do them. I wouldn't want to mother the way she mothered, but I think it would be great if she could have known my kids. I think if she were around that I would have a different relationship with her than I did as a child and would get something from her that I didn't get then. We would have a shared interest — the children — that we didn't have when she was alive."

If subtle ways, we may find ourselves grieving the loss of our mothers again, because her early death means our children and our mother will never know each other. Melissa wishes her mother could have seen her and her siblings as parents. She says, "When I think about this, which I do because I think about my mother every day, what makes me saddest is that my children will never know her. It's the life experience, the judgment, and the wisdom that she would have shared with them that's not happening. And in some ways, it's unfathomable to me that my mother, who was such a strong person and personality, is not someone my children will ever know directly. I think less about how she would have helped or the advice she would have offered (because I know she would have had a lot of advice), and more about how I miss her for me and I miss her for my children."

Melissa goes on, "I feel bad that my mother hasn't seen my siblings as parents, because they also had children after she was gone. Each of them is so completely into being a parent. It's their life. They love this. It would have been so great for my mom to see that, because she and my dad gave us that."

My In-Laws Feel More Like Family

Sometimes having a baby gives us a new sense of freedom with our in-laws.

Having a baby also brings our in-laws more into our lives. For many of us, we feel closer to our husband's parents. We share both our love for our child and the experience of being parents. We feel that our value goes up with them now that we are the mother of their grandchild! At the same time, babies can create stresses and strains with our relatives. Often our conflicts are a matter of style and family culture. And it may be more difficult for us to communicate about these differences because our in-laws are not *our* parents. These tensions need to be addressed so we don't jeopardize our children's chance to form a close relationship with our husband's family.

Sometimes having a baby gives us a new sense of freedom with our in-laws. Jocelyn describes how her relationship with her mother-in-law has improved now that she has a baby: "I have a mother-in-law with whom I've never had a good relationship. It's always been strained. When the baby was born, I dreaded her coming to visit. I was totally exhausted and the last thing I needed was to entertain her. On the other hand, this was her first grandchild, and I didn't want to deny her the chance to meet him. So she came to visit us, and it was fine. In fact, I felt I could be myself more and be much more honest with her. I felt like having a new baby gave me license to just be myself."

Having a baby may create new tensions with our in-laws. Barbara quit her job to be at home with her children. She has difficulty being with her mother-in-law who has a different set of values and experiences than she does. She says, "It's been hard for me because we spend a lot of time with my in-laws, and I don't always feel like my mother-in-law and I see things eye-to-eye. She had kids at age twenty-one and never worked before becoming a mother. She never saw the other side, what it was like to be on your own and work for a living. The most difficult thing for me about being a mother has been giving up my autonomy. I've really had a hard time with that and my mother-in-law doesn't understand it at all. Her interpretation of my struggle is that I'm being selfish."

Sometimes in-laws can be a source of support and comfort when our own parents can't be. As Greta, a mother of two, says, "One of the things that's been a big surprise for me is how uninterested my mother is as a grandmother. My kids are her only grandchildren, so I thought she'd be much more into spending time with them. That's been sad for me. But the great thing is that my husbands' parents are so involved. They have loads of grandchildren, and yet they couldn't be more excited and eager to spend time with our children. We're all lucky to have them in our lives."

Our relationship with our in-laws may require us to use our best negotiation skills. A mother of a two-year-old, Audrey talks about how she has worked out ways to be with her husband's parents so everyone feels satisfied: "Interacting with my in-laws has been a negotiation ever since our son was born. I've come to the realization that there isn't going to be any major character transformation on either side. We are 'givens.' So given who we are, I try to maximize the number of win-win situations for all of us. For instance, my mother-in-law babysits for me one morning a week so I can go to a class. It works out because she gets to see her grandchild and I get to do something I need to do. I also try to have my husband take responsibility for the communication with his parents. They like staying in touch with him, and I don't become the social secretary for the family."

Rebecca feels very lucky to have all four grandparents living near her. She says, "My in-laws recently moved near us to be closer to their grandchildren. My husband and I joke that it's great for the kids and tough on our marriage. But I grew up with four grandparents within five minutes of us, and I loved that. I really respect my parents, because whatever difficulties they may have had with their parents, they sheltered us from them. My parents never said a bad word about any of our grandparents. We always thought they were fantastic, and I want my kids to have that same kind of love and appreciation for their grandparents."

As Arthur Kornhaber writes in his book *Between Parents and Grandparents*, grandparents can be a great natural resource. They have an enduring attachment to our children and enrich our family life. They can help us through the trials and tribulations of new parenthood.[37] Yet figuring out how they will be involved in our family life can be a process. We need to let them know (in the nicest possible way) that we appreciate their involvement and suggestions, but we've decided to do things a little differently in our family. And at other times, it may mean asking them for more support. In any case, our children will treasure the time they spend with other people who love them as much as we do — and let them get away with more!

S I X

How Do We Mother Daughters and Sons?

A little girl is Innocence playing in the mud,

Beauty standing on its head and Motherhood drag-

ging a doll by the foot . . . . A little boy is Truth

with dirt on its face, Beauty with a cut on its finger,

Wisdom with bubble gum on its hair and the Hope

of the future with a frog in its pocket.

— *Alan Beck*

*Never before have humans, both male
and female, been challenged to stretch
to their full size. Nothing less than
strength, boldness, a sense of adven-
ture, insight, courage, and leadership
joined with gentleness, sensitivity,
caring, kindness, and understanding
will see us into the future.*
— Don and Jeanne Elium

Gender is a hot topic right from the start of our pregnancy.
Early on we begin wondering what it would be like to have a
baby girl or a baby boy. Some of us honestly don't care what
the sex of our child will be. Others of us do have a preference,
even if we don't admit it out loud. In fact, we may be disappointed when we find out the gender of our baby (through
amniocentesis or at delivery) if we don't "get" what we had
hoped for. But any unhappiness is short-lived because we
soon fall in love with our individual child. Like so much of
parenting, we learn to accept that our offspring's sex is something over which we have no control, and that it doesn't matter anyway, because we adore *this* baby.

Does the sex of our baby impact how we mother him or
her? As women who grew up with feminism, we are wary of
sexual stereotypes. In our own lives we have fought to do
whatever we put our minds to and have disregarded the

clichés about men's and women's "innate" abilities. Thus it is curious when we start noticing that little boys and little girls act differently. For years these "male" and "female" behaviors were thought to be a result of how a child was socialized. Now researchers are showing that there are differences between boys and girls that can't be explained by environmental factors alone. As mothers, the trick is to acknowledge and accept these differences while not limiting our children because of the biology with which they were born.

I Want a Daughter

We are comfortable with daughters because we have the same body and female identity.

Many of us spend our pregnancies longing to have a little girl. We want a daughter because girls are familiar to us. We are comfortable with daughters because we have the same body and female identity. If we are close to our mothers, we look forward to sharing this privileged relationship with a daughter of our own. We believe our daughter will be our friend and have visions of a lifetime of heartfelt chats over mugs of hot tea. We are excited about having girls in a world where women have so many choices and look forward to sharing our generation's advances with the next generation of women.

Positive experiences with female relatives may contribute

to our desire to have a girl. Cynthia, who has three daughters, talks about how much she wanted a girl. She describes how close she felt to her female relatives and how important it was to have that relationship with a daughter of her own. She says, "When I was pregnant the first time, people would ask me if I wanted a boy or girl, and I said I wanted a girl. It was so politically incorrect because you're supposed to say you just want a healthy baby. But I wanted a girl. I have such strong relationships with the women in my family, I thought I would be really disappointed if we didn't have at least one girl. When my first daughter was born and they told me she was a girl, I thought I'd died and gone to heaven. Three girls later, my prayers have been answered three times."

If we had sisters, we simply may feel more at ease with girls. Dana, who has a two-and-a-half-year old daughter, describes how she grew up in a family of girls and how comfortable she is in the company of females. She says, "I just love having a daughter. It's such a special bond. I'm sure I would have been happy with a boy, but I have sisters and come from a very girl-dominated home. We used to ask my father if he wished he'd had a boy and he would say, 'Are you crazy? What would I do, wish away one of my daughters?' So I grew up in a very healthy environment for girls. I think it's better that I have a daughter because I'm innately better at being around girls than I think I would be with boys."

Cecily has a two-year-old daughter. During her pregnancy, she hoped she would have a boy but is quite happy that she has a little girl. She expects that her own experiences as a girl and woman will help her to guide her daughter as she grows up. She says, "When I was pregnant I really wanted to have a boy. It wasn't a matter of having a boy first so there would be an 'older' brother, it was a matter of getting an 'obligation' out of the way. Although he wouldn't say it, I know my husband wanted to have a boy. When the ultrasound showed that this was not the case, I felt a little disappointed. Not that I wasn't thrilled about having a daughter, but I felt there would be more pressure on the next pregnancy. I adore being the mother of a daughter. I understand her so well. As she gets older, I have the confidence that I will understand the problems she will face and hopefully can help her make the right decisions and teach her to find her way in the world."

I Love Having a Son

For many, the bond with a little boy is affectionate and uncomplicated.

Many of us always knew we wanted a boy. Perhaps we have a sense that the firstborn should be male or that the oldest child should be a boy so any future siblings would have an older brother. We believe it is important for our husband to have a male child with whom he can have a close relationship. And we may like the idea of a son carrying on the family name.

Some of us have interests that are considered more "masculine" (like sports) and are eager to share those activities with a boy. We want to raise boys who have all the best male characteristics yet are also sensitive and caring. And others of us believe that it's easier to be male in our culture and don't want the worries associated with having a girl. For many, the bond with a little boy is affectionate and uncomplicated.

Our reason for wanting a son may be tied to our own childhood experience. Diane was adamant that she wanted a boy. She says, "I wanted a boy desperately. In my family, I was the oldest child and had a brother several years younger. I always thought it would have been great to have an older brother. Plus my mom died when I was young, and I never had that close mother/daughter relationship. I grew up without a strong woman mentor, and I wasn't sure I'd know how to be a role model to a girl. A boy seemed much easier to me, especially when he's a teenager. As an emotional teenager myself, I remember what a difficult time that was. I thought a boy would be more physical than emotional and easier to read. Being the mother of a son seemed less complicated than trying to raise a girl."

Polly wanted a boy because she knew how important it was to her husband. She says, "My main reason that I wanted a boy was that my husband really wanted a son. My husband was very nervous about having a girl, particularly a teenage girl. We found out before the baby was born that we were having a boy, and I was so relieved when they told us that I cried. I didn't want the stress of knowing my husband might be upset. I wasn't concerned at all about the energy level that a boy might have. I'm very athletic and knew I could keep up. In fact, I liked the idea of a child who was physical and out-going."

Sometimes we have to get over our initial disappointment before our son finds a very special place in our heart. Julia, the mother of a son, really wanted a girl during her pregnancy. She says, "I was desperate to have a daughter. My interests are so female that I knew I could relate to a girl. When I found out I was having a boy, I just kept saying to my husband, 'What will I *do* with a boy?' I couldn't imagine the kinds of activities we would share, and therefore it was hard to imagine having a relationship with a boy. One of the things that was so threatening to me about having a son was that I wouldn't be needed. I didn't want to have a baby to let him go. But I adore my son and can't imagine life without him. In fact, as much as I'd still very much like to have a daughter, I also feel a little sorry for my friends who won't have the sweet experience of being the mother of a little boy."

Having a son can change our perspective on life. Joanne remembers not being able to imagine having a son, as she comes from a family of three girls. Having two sons has changed her view of the world. She says, "When my first son was born, I would say I felt mildly disappointed, but that moment was so fleeting, I can't really recall it. Mostly I was enormously relieved to have given birth to a healthy boy. I now have two sons, and it's strange, although the 'girl' thing should feel more natural to me, it actually feels foreign. Now I find myself noticing boys in the world. This is a very hot topic for me, because I have often felt that mothers of girls feel somehow superior. Boys get such a bad rap. I'm having a blast raising sons, and I love having two children of the same sex. I find myself crusading for boys. I'm very protective of the male culture, a position I never thought I would be in."

I'm Glad I Have Both a Girl and a Boy

We like the idea that each parent will have the experience of raising a child who is "like us."

Many of us like the idea of having both a daughter and a son. As mothers of girls, we expect to enjoy the unique bond between mother and daughter. With sons, we relish the special relationship with an opposite-sex child. We like the idea that each parent will have the experience of raising a child who is "like us." We believe that our children will be comfortable with the opposite sex since they will be raised in a family that includes both girls and boys. For some of us, having "one of each" makes us feel that our family is "complete."

Having a girl and a boy gives us the chance to explore different types and aspects of relationships. Joyce finds that her relationship with her daughter is different than the one she has with her son: "I knew I wanted a girl, and I'm crazy about my daughter. I always felt that if I didn't have a girl in my life I'd be losing out on something, that wonderful mother/daughter relationship, which is both fulfilling and exasperating. It's a very full experience. But I'm also thrilled to have an opposite-sex relationship, because I have a really special relationship with my dad. I see how what goes on between my son and me is more like what has gone on between my father and me. There's tenderness between my son and me that's special. Maybe it's that our personalities are well suited to each other. My relationship with each child is very different. I have to believe it's a gender thing."

Ann Marie enjoys having a daughter and a son. She says, "It's nice to have both a girl and a boy. I'm really glad I've had the experience of mothering both. Sometimes I regret that my kids won't have a same-sex sibling because I think they'd be closer friends. What's great is that each of them will be comfortable with the other sex, because there will always be children around of both genders. Having girls and boys is different. With my daughter, I think of her as my little buddy. With my son, it's more like he's a small boyfriend."

For some of us, the gender of our children makes no difference. Eleanor, age thirty-six, has a son and a daughter under two years old. She didn't care whether she had girls or boys. She observes, "I've never had a preference for boys or girls. It's interesting because now that we have a boy and a girl, people will say to us, 'Oh, you have the perfect family.'

Where do they come up with that? I would be thrilled to have two boys. It would be great to have two girls. The perfect family is one in which all four of us can live peacefully together in the same household!"

Girls and Boys Are Different

But before the baby is even born, girl and boy brains begin developing differently, and children start to experience themselves as female or male very early in life.

With babies and young children it is difficult to determine whether certain behaviors are a result of gender, birth order, or individual personality. In many ways a baby is a baby, as girls and boys experience similar physical development until the age of seven. However, many a new mother has observed that little girls and little boys act differently. This gender-identified behavior is perfectly normal and begins showing at age three. Yet growing up in a feminist era, we're taken aback when we observe our children acting in ways that are so traditionally "girlish" or "boyish."

The consensus now is that gender does not always determine behavior but creates tendencies toward certain traits. Environment, socialization, and personality all play a role in who a child becomes. But before the baby is even born, girl and boy brains begin developing differently, and children start to experience themselves as female or male very early in life.[38] Our goal as mothers is to guide the development of our children's separate identities and to provide possibilities throughout their lives that are not constrained by their sex.[39]

My Daughter Only Wears Hot Pink

As early as two to four days after birth, girls are likely to pay attention to human faces longer and more intently than boys.

Although we believe that each child should be supported in finding her or his own path, we're often surprised to find that stereotypical "girlish" behavior is alive and well among our young daughters. The old adage that girls are interested in "people" and boys are interested in "things" seems to be born out by scientific observation. Researchers have shown that these tendencies start showing up within a few days of a newborn's life.

As Jeanne and Don Elium write in their book *Raising A Daughter*, girls define themselves in the context of their relationships with other people. As early as two to four days after birth, girls are likely to pay attention to human faces longer and more intently than boys.[40] Baby girls will look you in the eye longer and are generally less distracted.[41] Girls' brains are wired to receive and process information in a way that makes them more sensitive than boys in their very beings.[42] A preschool teacher with whom I spoke observed that by the time they are three, girls on average are more likely to develop one-to-one relationships with other children, are more conscious of peer relationships, and show greater interest in activities in which they interact with others. And while researchers have yet to uncover why the average three-year-old girl will only wear pink, many a new mother has had to live with the phenomenon on a day-to-day basis.

Having a sense of humor is often necessary as we deal with gender issues. Emily describes herself as a tomboy growing up. This is in contrast to her three-and-a-half-year old daughter who is very "female." Emily says, "Our efforts to raise our daughter in a gender-balanced environment are comical. We have trucks and blocks and dinosaurs, but her favorite toys are dolls and strollers to push them in. Her favorite color is fuchsia. She loves dresses, and it is a small miracle to get her into a pair of blue jeans. I've come to believe these characteristics come in the wiring."

But among girls, there are a wide variety of behaviors. The fact that not all girls fit the stereotypes is evidenced by Daphne's description of her four-year old identical twins. She describes how one daughter acts typically "girlish" while the other one does not and the importance of honoring that. She says, "They're both pretty rough-and-tumble gals. But one of them likes dolls and strollers and dress-ups, while the other daughter couldn't care less about that stuff. That daughter is totally physical, and as long as she's running or jumping or climbing, she's happy. I try to let each of them just be who they are."

My Son's First Word Was "Truck"

It has been documented that from infancy the average boy will have more aggressive tendencies and be more physically active than the average girl.

Michael Gurian writes in his book *The Wonder of Boys* that because of the dominance of the hormone testosterone, aggression and physical risk taking are wired into boys. It has been documented that from infancy the average boy will have more aggressive tendencies and be more physically active than the average girl.[43] By preschool boys are more likely to hit, play in groups rather than one-on-one, and choose toys such as trucks, swords, and guns. And generally boys are more competitive than girls and seek more physical play. They tend to have a less empathetic response to someone in pain and are more likely to be provocative in their initial interactions with others.[44]

Again, this does not mean that we should expect all boys to act this way, but that, on average, a boy will show some of these behaviors. Psychologist Evelyn Bassoff writes that mothers need to understand and accept this "boy energy" and make sure it's channeled in healthy ways.[45] Regardless of the research, how many of us are amazed at the ingenuity with which our sons can turn every object (including a Barbie doll) into a gun?

For those of us influenced by the feminist movement, our little boy's attraction to certain toys can baffle and amaze us. Serena explains that her two-year-old son was born with an orientation toward trucks and fire engines: "I know we didn't only give my son trucks when he was little. He had stuffed animals and puzzles, but he always loved the trucks. I don't know where that comes from, but then you reinforce it because you know what they like. But he started the whole thing. Even when he was very little, before he could even sit up, a fire truck would go by and he'd be beside himself with excitement. I know I didn't encourage that because I could care less about fire engines myself."

Sometimes boys can be physically challenging. Eve has two boys and a third on the way. She says, "Boys are very high energy, very physical. I don't know anything else because I only have boys, but I contrast my experience to that of my friends who have daughters, and it's different. They tell me about how their girls sit in the kitchen and read books while they cook dinner, or how they're happy to play in their room with their paints. That would never happen in my family in a million years. In my house, I always have to be on the alert for tumbling furniture."

Samantha is the mother of three boys who do not conform to the aggressive male stereotype. She says, "My boys are really easy. They're not aggressive. In fact, sometimes I think it might serve them well if they were a bit more aggressive, but I'd rather teach them to assert themselves than not to hit. My first son has never hit in his whole life, even out of frustration as a toddler. So he set the tone. The second one would have hit more but didn't, because the first one didn't hit back. The third one has a different temperament. He'll try and hit his brothers over the head just to see what their reaction is, but if they're not hitting back, it doesn't cause the excitement he's hoping to generate."

My Son and Daughter Don't Act the Same

For mothers that have both daughters and sons, we may try to treat our children the same, only to discover that girls and boys play differently, talk differently, and solve problems differently.

Evelyn Bassoff has written about the relationship between mothers and daughters and between mothers and sons. She says that raising girls and boys is different, and that as parents, we are wise to respect these differences.[46] For mothers that have both daughters and sons, we may try to treat our children the same, only to discover that girls and boys play differently, talk differently, and solve problems differently. Being conscious of these differences allows us to help each child express themselves in their own style.

Twins provide interesting insights into gender behavior. Heidi is the mother of five-month-old twins, one boy and one girl. She already sees differences between the two. She says, "We really try not to treat them differently, yet every gift we received when they were born was pink and blue. It's hard not to stereotype them because some of their behaviors are so classically 'boy' or 'girl.' In many ways, they came that way. My son is the more physical one. My daughter is much more quiet and thoughtful. My son bats away at toys in his crib. My daughter thinks about it, and thinks about it, and thinks about it, and finally reaches out and grabs an object. So some of the stereotypes are true. On the other hand, my son is much more sweet and cuddly than my daughter is. She's sweet too, but she's more distant. They haven't started playing with different toys yet, but we want to encourage both of them to play with whatever they want. It's too early to tell how they'll be and how we'll be with them."

Heidi continues, "I had sisters and we went to all-girl schools. Growing up, I really believed that I could do anything a boy could do. I'm tall, and for a while I was even taller than most of the boys. So even physically, I believed that I could do anything. I wonder whether my daughter will have that same feeling because she's growing up with a brother. She'll be aware of the differences much sooner. Right from the beginning, she'll see that her brother is bigger — he was bigger at birth. So it will be interesting to see whether she'll have the same level of confidence I did coming from an all-girl environment."

Are certain behaviors due to gender or personality? Often it's hard to tell. Rose talks about the differences between her three-year-old twins (one girl and one boy), yet can't say what "causes" these behavioral differences. She says, "My son has been the easier child. For instance, he could care less about his clothes, while my daughter cares a lot about what she wears. She's got it in her head that she will only wear pink. And recently she has to pack up her purse every time we go somewhere. (She could just be emulating me.) She doesn't like big groups and clings more to me in social situations, but I think my son's more attached to me. When he gives me a hug, he means it. I don't sense that as much with her. I don't know how much of this is their sex and how much is just who they are, but it's interesting to note the differences."

I Hope I'm Raising a Strong Daughter

The mother/daughter relationship is the foundation for our daughter's identity and sense of well-being.

As mothers of daughters, we hope to bring up girls who are strong and compassionate, assertive and respectful, self-reliant yet also able to have satisfying relationships with others. We hope to foster their self-esteem and support their pursuit of both family and career. We hope to broaden our daughters' preferences and behaviors and increase their options for development as women. At a young age, we do this by encouraging them to be physically active so they will gain confidence in their own strength, and by providing them with toys that allow them to develop problem-solving skills and creative thinking.[47] We try not to be too overprotective. And we tell them they're smart as well as pretty.

Bassoff writes that young girls develop within relationships and usually identify strongly with their mothers.[48] The mother/daughter relationship is the foundation for our daughter's identity and sense of well-being. By example we show them what it means to be female. Unlike our sons, little girls remain identified with their mothers even as they are acquiring autonomy. We try not to limit our daughter's activities to those that are traditionally female, yet it can be hard when all she wants to do is push her baby in a stroller, paint her fingernails, and dress up as a bride.

In raising our daughters, many of us seek to offer both "traditional" and "nontraditional" experiences. Amy, whose daughter is eight months old, talks about how she and her husband are already trying to create an environment that supports many sides of her daughter's personality: "I'm a very strong feminist and am very pro-female. I'm always trying to help young career women, so I really want to share my experiences with my daughter and help her through the difficult times. I object to girls being made to feel like the only thing they have to offer is their looks. Whenever we tell my daughter she's cute, we also try to tell her that she's strong and smart. I want her to take advantage of the good things about being female, of being attractive and coquettish and fun, but I also want her to have inner strength and resolve. I want her to be self-confident and athletic and able to operate on multiple levels."

Cynthia encourages her three daughters to pursue a variety of interests, not just those that are classically female. She also imparts to her daughters a sense of respect for her role as a stay-at-home mom. She says, "I try not to treat my daughters in a sexist way. My girls do traditional "girl" activities such as ballet, but they also play soccer. I try not to set limits on them but also let them do things that are girly. From time to time, my oldest daughter will say, 'Well, Mommy, you don't work. You don't have a job.' I tell her that Mommy went to school for a long time to be a doctor. I tell her I worked as doctor just like Daddy and now I work at home. My job is to be the best mother I can be. So I try to condition them and define for them what my role is and to provide some history about my life."

Our daughters may open us up to forgotten parts of ourselves. Having a daughter has given Grace a renewed appreciation for the feminine spirit. She observes, "My daughter is a real nurturer. Before I had a baby, I spent years in the business world building my more 'masculine' traits, so it's been eye-opening to have a daughter that's so 'female.' I look at what a nurturer she is and I think, you know, it's not such a bad thing to be compassionate and sensitive. I hope she will develop into someone who has a strong sense of herself, without losing those 'feminine' qualities of caring for and connecting with other people."

Celebrating rites of passage is an important way of nurturing our daughters. Janet feels that milestones should be acknowledged to provide a sense of meaning in a young girl's life. Although her girls are still quite young, Janet is starting to think about how to celebrate the important events throughout her daughters' lives. She says, "I think a lot about rites of passage. I went to a Bat Mitzvah recently and noticed what I liked and didn't like about it. It's still a long way away for my daughters, but I wonder, 'What is it that you want your thirteen-year-old daughter to have done and thought about? What do you want to do to set her up until the next milestone at age eighteen or twenty-one? What kinds of things are developmentally appropriate for girls her age to be thinking about and planning for?' By having these celebrations, a girl can learn about herself and see that she's important."

I Want to Raise a Compassionate Son

One of our tasks as the mother of a boy is to lay the groundwork for his perception of women.

Many of us want to raise sons who are strong and confident, yet also responsible, sensitive, and compassionate. We want them to respect women and be able to love and care for other people. And we definitely want them to be able to communicate. Sometimes we are uncomfortable with how physically active boys can be and wonder how we will manage all that energy. We worry that as mothers of boys, we will spend many anxious moments averting danger and making trips to the emergency room. Bassoff writes about the importance of trying to nurture and enjoy the physicality of boys. She says that our sons allow us to discover our own adventurous spirit and playfulness.[49]

Children of both sexes separate from their mothers, but it has a different meaning and time line for girls and boys. Because she is like her mother, a little girl remains identified with her mother even as she is acquiring her independence. A boy does not pattern himself after his mother but turns away, often toward a father or father figure.[50] This is a normal process that starts in early childhood and continues through adolescence. Psychologists such as Bassoff write that a mother can help her son separate by allowing him to return to her when he needs maternal nurturing. For mothers and sons, separating is a normal part of a relationship that doesn't need to be severed.

Raising a son gives us the opportunity to encourage the best of both male and female characteristics. Judy, whose son is four months old, says, "I've thought a lot about whether I'm a different mom to a son than I would be to a daughter. But I probably won't be able to tell you for another five years. I've talked to my mother about this, and she said she made a really conscious effort in the fifties and sixties not to treat me differently than my two brothers. Part of me sees raising a boy as this wonderful opportunity to raise a man who is sensitive and strong."

When given the chance, some boys enjoy both activities that are considered "male" and those that are not. Gabrielle talks about the range of behaviors her four-year-old exhibits: "In raising our son, both my husband and I have tried to be as gender neutral as possible. It is amazing how young they are when they start showing 'girl' or 'boy' behavior. Our son has dolls, trains, trucks, dress-up clothes, and paints, and loves them all. We encourage him to play with whatever strikes his fancy, except guns, which strike his fancy a lot. At age four, he's still in-between. He has male and female friends. He loves to play house and to play with his trains, although he tends lately to engage in more aggressive play more often. He recently announced that, 'Girls like pretty things and boys like tough things,' which he said while wearing his chef's hat, frying pan in hand. Our goal is to raise a sensitive man — one who realizes that there are differences between the sexes, but that both are equally respected."

One of our tasks as the mother of a boy is to lay the groundwork for his perception of women. Charlotte, who has two boys, says, "I love having boys. I'm relieved that I don't have to be their primary role model but that I can be a female role model to my boys. My husband and I have a pretty equal partnership. It's great for my sons to see a strong woman who has equal economic standing and responsibilities within the family. I can ski. I can run. I can work. Dad can cook. Dad can clean. Dad can do laundry. We try to raise them to be compassionate and to have an understanding of women too."

In female households, it's important to have solid male role models. Nancy, a lesbian mother of a son, knows the significance of creating a community that includes men to whom her son may turn as he begins to learn what it means to be male. She says, "It's a special challenge for a single parent raising an opposite-sex child, or a lesbian couple raising an opposite-sex child, or for a couple raising a child with a different ethnic or racial background. To allow the child to have opportunities to see themselves reflected in your adult friends is crucial. If they have questions, that may be the person they go to rather than the parent, because they may have an affinity for that person. They see that that person looks like them. I think it's important for kids to have people like them around them sometimes, even if it's just the body type. I want him to see men's bodies and see that they are different from women's bodies. If there's an awareness of that and a sensitivity to that on the part of the parents, the rest will fall into place."

Bassoff writes that boys court physical danger and bodily injury in a way that girls do not, especially in adolescence.[51] Sometimes our protective instincts make it hard for us to embrace our son's physical nature. Brenda says, "With a boy, I feel like I'm going to have to let go of my fear of him getting hurt. I don't think he'll be afraid of the world, but I'll be afraid for him. That's a huge challenge for me, to let go. How do you, as a parent of a boy, let him go and not let him get hurt? You don't want him to be afraid of the world. You don't want him to be a sissy. You want him to get out there but when he comes home with a swollen face because he fell on the playground, you feel terrible. I want to be calm about it. I recently saw a friend's daughter who had a huge scrape on her face from falling down, and I thought well, maybe that's just what happens when you're a kid."

Though we know it's necessary and right, it can be hard to think about letting our sons go. Julia fears her son separating from her. She hopes to maintain a close relationship with him despite the normal separation process that occurs as boys grow older. She says, "Separation is my biggest fear. It's necessary for my son's growth — I know I have to embrace it — but it's going to be the hardest thing for me. I find it such a painful thought that part of my job is to embrace a loss of intimacy for a period of time and be glad for it. Theoretically it will come back again but in a really different way. I've read a lot about having sons, and one of the ideas that really resonated with me was the notion that even though a boy must separate from his mother, it's equally important to stay connected and not let him turn inward and shut down emotionally. I can teach my son where it's appropriate to live by the masculine rules but also create a place at home where it's still okay to cuddle and be in a relationship. I want to avoid raising another generation of men who are emotionally cut off."

I Want to Bring Up Happy Children

*As women who live in a time when traditional roles for women
and men are in flux, we want to raise our children in a
nonsexist way.*

Perhaps it's easiest for mothers of both daughters and sons to
make contrasts between girls and boys and to determine
whether we treat them differently. Mothers of both girls and
boys attributed some of their children's behavioral differences
to gender and other differences to personality and birth order.
Many of us feel that a child can do or be anything with the
right support and nurturing. Therefore we hope to provide
our children with equal opportunities and encouragement. At
the same time, when our children act in ways that are typically "boyish" or "girlish," we may find ourselves reinforcing
the behavior, often unintentionally.

Ann Marie has a three-and-a-half-year old daughter and a
one-and-a-half-year old son. She says, "I do treat my daughter and son differently. I have a degree in education so I
should know better. So much of it has to do with my expectations of them. I expect my daughter to be cooperative and
better behaved. Recently a friend and I took our daughters to
a restaurant for tea. We mothers talked while the two little
girls sat there happily and kept each other entertained. I probably wouldn't do something like that with my son because I

don't have the expectation that he would be able to sit still and enjoy it. And the other thing is that I don't know if I'd really want my son to be calm and quiet and enjoy a tea party in a fancy restaurant."

Ann Marie continues by contrasting her sense that she will always be close to her daughter with her feeling that her time with her son is "limited." She says, "With my daughter, I feel like she'll be there forever. With my son, I feel like I have to get my hugs in now, because I won't always be able to do that with him. He's very sweet and affectionate — maybe even more so than my daughter was at his age — but I know at age six, he's not going to want to kiss me good-bye when he goes off to school."

Do we love our sons differently than we love our daughters? Before having her third baby, a son, Monica was worried that she wouldn't be as close to him as she is to her two older children who are girls. She says, "I am absolutely crazy about that little boy in a way I never would have imagined. It is true that mothers fall in love with their sons in a way that is very different from loving daughters. I also have fewer concerns with him. With the girls, I struggle with how to make them strong but still feminine, how to help them grow into the kind of women that will be happy and successful in whatever ways they choose. With our son, I simply adore him. Somehow it becomes his father's job to make him strong and masculine. I simply get to snuggle with him and make him laugh. What a joy!"

Treating our children differently is sometimes due to other people. Polly, who has a two-and-a-half-year-old son and a newborn daughter, says it's hard not to raise your children differently in part because you're not the only influence on them. She relates, "It starts as early as when they receive baby gifts. People buy toys that are more boyish or girlish depending on what gender child you have. Yet part of their behavior is just who they are. My son's always loved balls and buses, and his first word was 'truck.' And even though I don't want to start treating them differently, just the other day I was going through my son's clothes to see what my daughter could wear and already I found myself thinking, 'I don't want to put her in that, it's too masculine.' It's really too early to say how I'll be as a mother to the two of them, but I'm trying to be very equal. Basically I hope my kids will be successful and happy and that they will be able to do whatever they want to do."

As women who live in a time when traditional roles for women and men are in flux, we want to raise our children in a nonsexist way. Even at an early age, we can begin to sensitize them to the gender biases so prevalent in our culture. Yet in addition to social influences, much of who our baby becomes is determined by early differences in body chemicals, brain development, and hormones. While not accepting the stereotypes about what girls and boys should do or who they might become, we can acknowledge the differences and use this knowledge to channel their behavior in suitable ways. As parents, we must try to raise children without prejudices, yet also realize that some of their behavior just comes pro-grammed in their genes. In other words, it's not necessarily a setback for feminism if our young daughter's favorite outfit is a frilly tutu or our three-year-old son is fascinated by the workings of a backhoe.

SEVEN

We're Ready to Have More Children, Aren't We?

This time I had done nothing. I had heard that second births were easy — you practically just dropped by the hospital and picked up your baby. Besides, I knew all about childbirth having been through it one whole time.

— Adair Lara

With our first child, we insisted he finish his spinach before he got raisins. With the second child, we were just happy if he finished his french fries before he ate candy.
— A mother of three

So now that we've got being a mother down, we've decided it's time to have another child. Even though we knew what to expect, our pregnancy was harder the second time. We'd forgotten how much sleep deprivation affects our mood. We spent the months before the second baby was born feeling guilty that we were displacing our first child. Now that the new baby is here, our beloved first child is being so contrary that we're not sure we even like her anymore. Was this really a good idea?

On the other hand, the birth and labor of our second wasn't as scary because we knew what to expect. We're much more relaxed as mothers. It's a lot less nerve-wracking to take care of a newborn the second time. Plus our lifestyle is already oriented toward children, so the overall adjustment is not as great. Besides, we'd forgotten how sweet an infant can be. And during those moments when our older child is being loving and affectionate with the new baby, we think they might actually become friends some day. Okay, maybe we weren't completely nuts to have done this.

I'm Thinking about a Second Child

*A sibling is someone with whom our first child can play, learn
to negotiate, share the family traditions, and ultimately, gang
up on us as parents.*

What prompts us to have a second child? Because 80 percent
of American families include two or more children,[52] our concept of family often includes more than one child. And as
older mothers, we may start thinking about having a second
baby soon after the arrival of the first. Many of us choose to
have a second baby because we don't want our first child to be
alone. Or perhaps we want the chance to raise both a boy and
a girl. We believe our child will benefit from having a brother
or sister. A sibling is someone with whom our first child can
play, learn to negotiate, share the family traditions, and ultimately, gang up on us as parents. Often our expectations
about optimal spacing drive the timing of our second child.

Because we were older when we had our first child, our
age is a major consideration in the decision to have a second
child. Wendy has an eighteen-month-old daughter and is ten
weeks pregnant with her second baby. She says, "Ideally, I
would have liked to have them further apart, but I'm thirty-
seven and my husband is forty and we felt like we weren't
getting any younger. So it got to the point where they would
be two years apart and I convinced my husband to go ahead

and try to have a second baby. I argued that our daughter shouldn't be an only child. She wouldn't have anyone to play with. We could end up being a big burden on her if she has to take care of us in our old age by herself."

Some of us always knew we would have more than one child. Emily has two children who are three years old and nine months old. She says, "We always thought we would have at least three children. I love family and chaos and togetherness. We didn't know what the age difference of the children should be or what we wanted. We didn't have things that planned out. We had our first daughter, and eighteen months later we both felt like we were ready for child number two. As for child number three, we will wait for the moment to strike us. I would have a flock of children if pregnancy suited me and I thought it was the socially responsible thing to do."

Being Pregnant Isn't As Much Fun the Second Time

The good news about second pregnancies is that for most of us delivery and labor are faster and easier.

There are a few fortunate women who find their second pregnancies easier than their first. More commonly, however, being pregnant with our second child is more difficult. Most of us "show" sooner. We have morning sickness more often and longer. Our backs ache more, and our varicose veins are more pronounced. And one of the hardest things is that we don't feel as special and cosseted as we did during our first pregnancy. It's more difficult to put our feet up or take catnaps when we are also trying to manage a small child, not to mention a partner, a household, and in many cases, a job.

Our second pregnancy is often quite different from the first. Eve says, "I didn't even have time to think about being pregnant the second time around. The first time I felt like I was a special creature and I had this wonderful secret. And the second time, I was so frazzled and preoccupied, it was only when I put on clothes and they didn't fit that I'd think, 'Oh, that's right, I'm pregnant.' I was just getting through the day."

Being pregnant can change the way we interact with our first child. Stacey has a two-year-old and just had her second baby. She describes the difficulty in being physical with her older child when she was pregnant: "One of the things I found hard about being pregnant was not being able to play with my daughter in the last few months. She had a little house that she loved to play in, and I was so big I couldn't get in it. Lifting her was hard, so even changing her was a problem. Getting her in the crib was hard. The thing I love most about not being pregnant anymore is that I get to be more physical with her again. I get to pick her up and hug her and throw her around and do the stuff she likes to do. That was a hardship for me during the pregnancy because I felt as if it created distance between my daughter and me."

Sometimes our second pregnancy has unexpected benefits for the first child. Dana has a two-and-a-half-year-old daughter and is three months pregnant. She says, "I've been totally exhausted. I've found that being pregnant has helped my daughter in her independence. Instead of carrying her as much as I did, I let her take over a little bit more. Now when she says, 'Uppie, uppie,' I say, 'Well, let me show you how to do this yourself.' Instead of carrying her down the stairs, we walk down. It's a slower process, but that's fine because I need to move more slowly, and it's good for her developmentally."

The good news about second pregnancies is that for most of us delivery and labor are faster and easier. Just knowing what to expect the second time can reduce many of our concerns. As second-time mothers, we are generally less worried about labor and delivery, although if our first birth was hard, we may be anxious that it will be difficult again. As Doreen, a mother of three says, "With my first baby, I had false labor for two weeks before the baby was born. It was back labor so it was very painful, and I was terrified. I kept wondering if this was the real thing. If false labor was so bad, what on earth was real labor going to be like? The real labor was like the false labor except it kept going and at the end of it, I got this beautiful baby. The second time, I wasn't afraid because I knew I would get through it. With the first one, I didn't know if labor was just going to go on forever and it would be a huge farce and I'd end up with a big watermelon instead of a baby. With the second, I knew what to expect, although I hadn't anticipated how fast it would happen."

I Can't Get Pregnant Even Though I Already Have One Child

The condition known as "secondary infertility" is described as occurring when a couple who has previously conceived is unable to do so again after trying for a period of two years.

Many of us who had no trouble conceiving and having a baby the first time find it harder to get pregnant with the second. For some of us, it just takes longer, but for others, getting pregnant the second time may require medical intervention. The condition known as "secondary infertility" is described as occurring when a couple who has previously conceived is unable to do so again after trying for a period of two years. An estimated 1.4 million couples are affected by secondary infertility.[53] In addition to age and length of time between births, secondary infertility can be caused by a variety of factors including complications experienced during labor and delivery, and either partner's general health, use of medications, or surgery.[54] Sometimes the reason is never ascertained, but not being able to get pregnant is painful as we try to make our dream of family life a reality.

Trying to get pregnant with our second can be hard on us emotionally. Penny was thirty-four when she had her first child and thirty-seven when she became pregnant with her second child. She says, "Getting pregnant with our first was a breeze. We were surprised when it happened right away. I was working hard and both my husband and I were traveling a lot, so the circumstances were hardly ideal for conception. With the second baby, it took me a year to get pregnant. I had quit my job and wasn't traveling anymore, so even though I was caring for a toddler, I felt that my life was less stressful. Maybe it was because I was two years older that it took longer. Anyway trying so long to get pregnant was an emotional roller-coaster ride. I kept wondering, 'Why us? Maybe we should just be happy with the one beautiful child that we have.' We were just about to see an infertility doctor when we finally got pregnant."

If we have expectations about the spacing of our children, we may feel even more anxious when we don't get pregnant. A mother of two, Laura discusses the disappointment of not being able to get pregnant with her second when she had hoped: "We had planned to have our children two years apart, but they ended up being almost four years apart because I had trouble getting pregnant with the second. With the first one, I didn't really care when I got pregnant. If it happened right away that was okay and if it didn't that was okay too. But with the second, I got really stressed out about the timing because I had this set idea of how far apart I wanted them to be. I wanted them to be close together in age so they would be friends. Everything turned out fine and they are friends despite the age difference, but it was really hard during those years that I didn't get pregnant."

When we can't get pregnant the second time, some of us try fertility treatments. Roxanne has a four-old and is six months pregnant. She says, "We tried to get pregnant for a while without success, so I started fertility treatments. It took a year and a half from the time we started the treatments until we got pregnant. And we kept trying different things from drugs to in-vitro fertilization. It was not fun — and it was expensive. Going to the monthly appointments with the infertility specialist was awful. I can't think of a place that's worse, except maybe a cancer ward. It was hard to sit in the waiting room with all these unhappy couples. And I kept wondering whether my older child was picking up on my anxiety. But in the end, it was worth it. We're so thrilled to be having a second baby."

Ellen is sad about having trouble conceiving a second child but says it's made her more grateful for her first child: "We've been trying to get pregnant with our second child for a long time and are going to an infertility doctor. Not being able to become pregnant has been hard, but it has also made me much more thankful for my daughter. Although I'd love to have another baby, I feel so blessed that we have one wonderful child. I appreciate her so much more because I know how lucky we are to have a child at all."

How Can I Love the Second Child As Much?

*During our second pregnancy, many of us begin to feel
nostalgic for the relationship we have with our first child.*

Many of us wonder whether we can care for our second child
as much as our first. We love our first child so intensely, we
can't imagine how we could ever love anyone else in the same
way. We worry that having a new baby will damage the special relationship we have with our first child. Janine describes
it this way: "My son is almost two years old and the thought
of having another baby is hard. How can I bring another child
home? I'd feel like I was cheating on my son. And my son was-
n't a planned baby. I didn't work to have him. He was a surprise. But I wonder what I will do. Will I like the second one
as much as I like the first one? Can I really like the second one
at all? How can I love another child like I love my son?"

During our second pregnancy, many of us begin to feel
nostalgic for the relationship we have with our first child. We
feel sad that we won't always have that exclusive relationship
and that by bringing a new person into the family we will
cause our first child to feel jealous and resentful. Mary Anne
describes it this way, "My children are twenty months apart.
When I found out I was pregnant with the second one, I was
really pretty depressed for a couple of weeks. It wasn't because
I was sad about having another baby because we wanted to

have another one and we wanted it then. I felt such a huge sense of loss because I felt that the special time I was going to have, just my daughter and me, was vanishing. It wasn't going to be there anymore and it was a very difficult thing to get over. Even though I was happy to be pregnant, there was a little part of me throughout my pregnancy that was sad. Once the baby came, it wasn't an issue anymore. You just have to remind yourself that you're giving your oldest child the greatest gift you can, which is a sibling."

"The way I look at it," says Lucy who is pregnant with her second child, "first you're single and then you meet someone and fall in love and you get married and your life is so much better. Then you have a baby and it gets even better. Then you have another baby and it's just that much richer. It's wonderful the way each new person in your family enriches your life."

Mothering Two Is Hard Work

Not only is it difficult for us to meet the physical requirements of two young children, but there's also the challenge of providing love and support to two different people.

There's no question that caring for two small children is a lot of work. Attending to the demands of a newborn is exhausting when we focus *all* our energy on the task. Sometimes it feels impossible when we also have an older child who is used to having our undivided attention. Not only is it difficult for us to meet the physical requirements of two young children, but there's also the challenge of providing love and support to two different people. Many of us are surprised that our second child isn't exactly like the first, and we find it difficult to switch gears and be emotionally available for children with different personalities and needs. In those first few months, we may start feeling that we aren't being as good a mother as we'd like to be with either child.

Few would characterize the first few months as a mother of two as "easy." Valerie's children are three and one. She remembers how difficult it was to have a newborn and a toddler: "It's important to focus on the fact that your kids are going to be okay, especially in the first few months when you feel like you're not meeting anybody's needs. I felt like a failure in every department. I would be trying to nurse the baby, while my toddler was trying to get my attention by lying on the floor pretending he was hurt. I felt like I just couldn't do anything right. It took me a while to get it together. I think you have to remember to not be too hard on yourself."

Though things may get off to a rocky start, they do get better — sometimes much better. Denise has a three-and-a-half-year-old daughter and a four-month-old son. When asked how things were going as a mother of two, she replied, "The first two months were hell. I didn't feel like I was doing a very good job with either child. It was hard having a newborn, and my older daughter totally regressed. I think she felt that if she weren't a baby I wouldn't love her anymore. A lot of her behavior has evened out, so it's much better now. In fact, having two children is more than twice as good. I've never had so much joy in my life."

With two children under two, Stacey discusses how knowing what to expect and having a support system in place have made having her second baby easier than the first: "I just spoke with a friend who recently had her first baby, and she was talking about how isolated she felt. That's a very common feeling that I didn't have with my second because of all the associations with other mothers that I've established from the first one. I was prepared for it the second time, so the isolation didn't happen. And my first birth was so difficult that to have a normal delivery the second time made me ecstatic for the first few months of my second baby's life."

Those of us who have twins have many of the same issues trying to respond to the physical and emotional needs of two children at the same time. Heidi has twins who are five months old. She says that one of the benefits of having twins is that you don't worry about whether they're behaving "normally" because they are different from birth. She says, "I have panic attacks but not very often. I don't spend a lot of time wondering whether what they are doing is normal because, with two, they do different things at different times. You realize quickly that they have different eating and sleeping patterns; there is no norm. I figure if I feed them and play with them and love them and do some basic things, they're going to be okay."

My Older Child Is Acting Out

And we should remember that in the long run, the pleasures of having a sibling outweigh the upsets and jealousies.

The arrival of a new baby is always hard for our older child. At first the older child may ignore the new baby, but at some point, she realizes that her perfect world has been shattered by the arrival of her sibling. That's when the older child may start acting in ways that are particularly diabolical. Caring for an older child can seem a lot harder than meeting the comparatively simple needs of a newborn. As moms, we are torn between feeling traitorous for displacing the older child and feeling infuriated by her antics. We must remind ourselves that our older child's moods and tantrums are normal and not a result of our being inadequate mothers. We must do what we can to be sensitive to our older child's need for familiar routines and extra attention from Mommy and Daddy — even if it's the last thing we have the energy to do. And we should remember that in the long run, the pleasures of having a sibling outweigh the upsets and jealousies.

Mothers with more than one child can be a great source of wisdom. Pregnant with her third child, Eve says, "Somebody said something to me that I thought was really valuable. They said, 'No matter what, the baby is going to get so much one-on-one attention that the person who really needs you is the older child. So whenever you can, you should really focus on the older child.'"

We may respond differently to having two children than we expected. Cheryl was surprised by her reaction to her first child, who was always competing with the baby for her attention. She says, "I experienced sadness about the second baby coming and losing the special relationship with my older son. But once the baby came, there were times when I didn't want to be with my older child even though I'd always adored the ground he walked on before. I had been worried about not possibly loving the second as much as the first. But when I was nursing and my older child would come over and say, 'Hold me, hold me, hold me,' it was really hard. It made me feel awful. I didn't know anyone with two kids, so I thought I was the only one who ever felt that way. It would have been nice to know in advance because I made it worse by thinking I was a horrible mother for having such negative feelings about my son."

Many mothers find that as their second child reaches certain developmental milestones — such as smiling, sitting up, or walking — they receive more attention from the adults around them and pose more of a threat to the first child. Lindsey describes this phenomenon: "I have kids who are eighteen months apart. My son is two and a half and my daughter is one. When the baby went from being immobile to sitting up and moving around, my son had a crisis. In the beginning things were great and my son didn't seem to take much notice of his new baby sister. But when my daughter turned six months old and started to participate more, my son had a really hard time. He was very cranky and had a lot of temper tantrums because he saw that she was more than just a baby doll. I didn't know what to do. Finally I consulted a family counselor about him. She assured us that his behavior was normal and that he needed to develop his language skills so he could talk about his feelings more. But it was a rough time for him — and for me."

My Second Child Isn't Just Like the First

Many of us are concerned about being fair to both children.

The relationship with the second baby isn't the same as the exclusive one-to-one relationship we had with our first baby. It's difficult to re-create those first months of motherhood when it was just the baby and us in our own little world. The second time around, the first child's life goes on with its schedules and routines, and the baby's needs are worked in around that. However, there are benefits to the second child of our being experienced moms. Usually we are more comfortable as parents. We know what to expect and our lives are already geared toward children. With a second child, we see that differences among children are normal and aren't the result of our doing something wrong as mothers. Instead of worrying about crib death or the baby meeting the proper developmental landmarks, we can really savor the baby phase.

Isn't it a relief to actually be relaxed with a newborn? Pam has a four-year-old and a new baby. She enjoys having an infant as an "experienced" mom. She says, "I'm starting all over again, but it's easy because I'm less nervous. I'm so much more relaxed because I know what I'm doing. With my first, if he made a squeak, I'd pick him up. To this day, he can't sleep through the night. By the time I had the second child, I'd learned that babies are resilient creatures, so I take my cue from my daughter instead of trying to figure out what to do by reading books. As a result of my being more relaxed, she seems like a more relaxed child."

We learn quickly that no two children are the same. Doreen, who has three children, says, "The bond that I, like most of the mothers I know, had with my first child was so intense because I had just one child. There was nobody interfering. We're so focused on the first child and know them so intimately because of that. With the second child, you don't have as much attention to give. You don't have as much time. The second child also has a different personality than the first, so you can't just transfer everything that you've already learned to your second child. Your relationship is very different."

Many of us are concerned about being fair to both children. This can be hard as our children's personalities emerge, and we realize that we get along differently with one child than the other. At times we may even like one child more than the other. Louise talks about the importance of being aware of not playing favorites: "My initial concern was how my first child would treat the younger one. How was I going to prevent the older one from being mean to the second one? I hadn't anticipated the opposite dynamic. As they've gotten older, I see that the younger one can be mean to the older one. Dealing with that has been a challenge because it's really important to me that they get along. I want them to love and respect each other. I'm really careful about not picking sides. I have to be self-conscious about how I intervene and respond to each child's individual characteristics."

My Husband Is More Involved

Happily, many women said that their husbands played a more active parenting role with the second child.

There's nothing like the joy of having a new baby in the house, but having a second child is draining for both mothers and fathers. It's harder on our relationship because (surprise!) two children are even more demanding than one. As parents, we find we get fewer "breaks" than when we had just one child and could take turns relieving each other. As mothers trying to nurture two small children, we may not feel that we're getting the nurturing we need from our partners. At the same time, our husbands may feel that they're the odd man out when the second baby arrives. They also may experience more financial pressure as the family expands. These kinds of issues are best addressed by spending time together and talking them out, even if it means hiring a baby-sitter to do it.

Happily, many women said that their husbands played a more active parenting role with the second child. In part, the work a second child creates requires our partners to be more involved. But second-time fathers also may feel more relaxed with an infant and more comfortable in their role as a parent. Often our husbands find that they become closer to the older child because they spend more time together while we mothers focus on the new arrival.

Our relationship with our husband may change yet again with the arrival of another baby. Kelly has daughters who are five and three, and remembers how her relationship with her husband was impacted by their second daughter's birth: "The dynamics changed almost immediately with the arrival of our second. My husband and I were separated by the need for one-on-one attention to the kids, and my older child felt the pain of not having our undivided attention all the time. The second child put the most strain on our relationship as a couple. My husband was already feeling left out and having two children made it worse. We have had to make a huge effort to provide time in our lives for each other. I think we don't do it enough but as the children get older it gets easier."

Just as we put effort into our relationships with our children, we also need to put effort into our relationships with our husband. Camille has two children who are just over a year apart. She says it's been hard on her marriage but stresses the importance of staying connected to her husband. She observes, "You have to touch base during this phase in your relationship or there won't be a forever. You have to set aside time for your relationship. You have to have a connection or else it's very difficult to regain that when your kids are older and you're finally able to spend time together again. With two small kids, we really have to make an effort to do that."

We've Decided to Have Just One Child

It's important to be very grounded and to have a broader community for your child so it's not just you in his or her life.

There are eighteen to twenty million only children living in the U.S.[55] Although there is a stereotype that only children are lonely or spoiled, research does not bear this out. As Ellie McGrath writes in her book *My One and Only*, parents and children of one-child families have been shown to have a high level of satisfaction with family life.[56] Although we might not have more than one child because of our age, health, or financial concerns, some of us choose to have one child because it allows us to focus our parental energy. We are able to spend more time with that child and to form a close relationship with him or her. As parents of one, there is less strain on our marriage and less of a financial burden. The disadvantages include not having a built-in playmate for our child and not having the chance for our child to develop the social skills that come from constant interaction (some would say "fighting") with siblings.

Some of us always thought we would have more than one child, but change our minds — for a variety of reasons, including age. Gina had her daughter at age forty. She had planned to have more children but doesn't want to "risk it" now that she's forty-three. She talks about the benefits of having one child: "I was very lucky to have a child at age forty and have it go so smoothly. When I imagined having children, I imagined having at least two, maybe three, but I got a late start. I do love the idea of having one child, because I can give him all my attention and really focus on him. I think it's made him feel secure and confident. And I wonder if I could have another child without being totally exhausted. It does make a difference when you become a mother at a later age."

One child may be enough for some of us. Alicia has a daughter who is two-and-a-half-years-old. Being the parent of one child works well given all the other demands in her family's life. She says, "My husband and I are set on having one child. It was a gradual decision. Before we had her, we thought we would have four, then once we had a child, we thought we'd have two and it went down from there. The balance of two careers, all the other things we want to do, and one child works for us as a family. We're afraid to throw another child into the mix. Not having a sibling is a sacrifice. I feel torn about that, but I know she'll get a lot more parental attention. It feels really right to us and our daughter seems very happy."

Stephanie also feels that having one child is the right balance for her and her partner. She discusses the unique considerations faced by the parents of an only child: "I feel strongly that our plate is full. I want to be able, financially and emotionally, to give him the very best lifestyle that we can. I do believe there are special issues as parents of an only child. It's important to be very grounded and to have a broader community for your child so it's not just you in his or her life. It's important for an only child to have a strong sense of community because they don't have it within their own family. Also the parents need to have a sense of limits in terms of what is provided so the child is raised feeling they are important but they don't run everything. They still have to share. They still have to make sacrifices. They still have to recognize the needs and interests of others. I think you can establish that in only children just as you do in children with siblings — it just may be more of a challenge."

I Want a Big Family

We may choose to have a larger family because we relish the joys of motherhood and the satisfaction of creating a family of our own.

Some of us choose to have three or more children. Often we grew up in large families ourselves and have a love of commotion and activity. Or maybe we were raised in a small family and always wanted to be part of something bigger. We like the idea of our children having brothers and sisters to serve as friends, confidants, and role models.

Some of us just didn't feel "done" as mothers of two and decide to have another child while we still can. Samantha, the mother of three, describes her decision to have a third child this way: "I thought I wanted two. I know all the advantages of having two children, but when I had two I didn't feel done. I compare it to flower arranging: with two it just seemed 'off.' I don't know why. There was no rational reason. (When you think about it, there's no rational reason to have any.) I'm not really an emotional person. I usually lead with my brain, but in this situation I led with my heart. I just couldn't shake the desire to have another child."

We may choose to have a larger family because we relish the joys of motherhood and the satisfaction of creating a family of our own. Cynthia says, "We thought we would have two kids, but when the second one turned two, we started thinking about having another. The desire to have a third became greater when my mother, who had lived close to us, moved away. It was then that I realized that the family I've created is primary. It was a real shift from seeing myself as part of my mother's family. I wanted to make my own family bigger because I thought it would be more fun. I also think motherhood is empowering and joyful and really the most important thing in the world, so I wanted to have another baby."

Many of us feel that there are advantages for our children in having more than one sister or brother. Allison, a mother of four, explains the benefits to her children of having many siblings. She says, "I'm doing this for them. In a small family, I think I could really spoil my kids. With four, that won't happen. I think it's important for them to develop a sense of self-sufficiency and competence. With brothers and sisters, my children will develop good coping skills. They'll have these wonderful close relationships with each other, because there's nothing like the bond between brothers and sisters. I also had this stupid fear that I might lose a child. It's irrational, but I couldn't have had just a couple kids because I would have worried about that. We had them close together so they would experience the friendship part of the sibling relationship. They may have different relationships with each other over time, but in the end they'll always be there for each other."

Are We Really "Done"?

The number of children we have impacts our family dynamics, our time, and our finances — not to mention the type of car we drive!

How do we know when we are "done" having babies? Some of us are very clear that we have the family size we want and that it works for us. Others are more ambivalent about being "finished." Even when we make the decision that we don't want any more children, we often feel wistful about our choice. We experience a sense of loss knowing that we won't experience a new life growing inside of us or the delights of having a new baby in the family. Having a baby around makes us feel young. Although we know we don't want to start over now that we're regaining some independence, we still may be reluctant to give away our baby clothes or sell the crib because we're sad about saying good-bye to this family-making phase of our lives.

Kathleen, the mother of two children ages five and two and a half, thought she was finished having babies until recently when she's started thinking about it again. She says, "I thought I was certain that I didn't want any more children, but I'm going through an ambivalent phase about maybe having a third. My youngest is almost three, so there's part of me that wants to have a baby around again. But the other side of that is that now that she is older, it's hard to imagine going back to the level of disarray in your life when there's a new baby around. My kids are at an age now where they're really fun and I'm able to do more with them. But I think I'll always long for a baby. I don't know when I'll feel totally resolved."

Often when it comes to ending our child-bearing, our heart fights with our head. Linda has two children who are four and a half and two and a half. She says, "The fact that my child bearing is done is a big issue for me right now because my husband had a vasectomy. I knew in my head it was the right thing. But my heart and my womb were saying something else. This happened a year ago and I'm still feeling the effects of it. Now I look around and see people with two daughters the same age as ours and a new baby, and that pulls at my heartstrings. I wonder when that goes away. I wonder if other mothers feel that way. There's an element to it that keeps me young. It's just that having babies is so powerful."

While some wrestle with a longing to have more children, others are confident in their decision to keep their family at its current size. Kelly says that two children is the right number for her and her husband: "I know I don't want to have another baby right now. As my children get older, I really look forward to what's to come. They get more and more interesting all the time. I loved them when they were babies, but I find this stage much more engaging. With two children, my husband and I can each take care of one of them if they need attention from an adult, yet they also have the benefit of having someone their own age to play with. I feel so lucky and grateful to have two beautiful healthy children. I wouldn't want to risk having a third and have something go wrong. Two is great for us."

For most of us, having children is a matter of choice — and what could be a bigger choice? The number of children we have impacts our family dynamics, our time, and our finances — not to mention the type of car we drive! We all know that a new baby brings additional pleasures and additional heartaches into our lives. And with the arrival of another child, each member of the family must go through an adjustment period. As we are trying to reestablish our equilibrium, we can take comfort in knowing that older children have turned against their siblings from the beginning of time and that babies have somehow managed to survive. When we're not cautioning our older child to "be gentle with the baby," we find ourselves actually enjoying our expanding family. Before we know it, we can't imagine what life would be like without the new addition.

Yet despite the joys of having a baby, there comes a point at which we know we won't be having any more. This can be a bittersweet realization. We may feel both sad that our baby-making days are over and also eager for the next exciting phase of parenthood.

E I G H T

Motherhood Is a Spiritual Journey

In my dealing with my child,

my Latin and Greek, my

accomplishments and my

money stead me nothing; but

as much soul as I have avails.

— Ralph Waldo Emerson

*Being the best possible parent you can
be means being the best possible person you can be; if that's not the purpose of a spiritual practice, what is?*
— Phil Catalfo

Many new mothers described having a baby and raising a
child as an opportunity for personal and spiritual growth.
Although some of us explored our spiritual formation in our
twenties, becoming parents forces us to look at our fundamental values and beliefs. As mothers, we are challenged to be
our best selves because children provide a mirror that allows
us to see who we really are — whether we like it or not. By
giving so much to someone else, we find ourselves becoming
more aware of who we are and what we stand for. Having children shows us the depth of our love, compassion, and understanding, in part because babies and children are so loving
and forgiving toward us. Many of us find that as we nurture
our children, they in turn nourish us.

Having a child is a gift that enhances and enriches our
lives. And in spite of the mundane nature of many of the tasks
associated with caring for a baby or small child, we often
experience a profound sense of gratitude and emotional fulfillment. Children push us to find our inner wisdom and the
strength to face down our dark moments. In contrast to the
directed, independent lives we forged as career women, hav-

ing a baby shows us that we are not always in control and that it's okay to turn to others for help. We try to be less judgmental of others when we realize how hard it is to be a mother, much less a "perfect" one. And when we are with small children, we learn to slow down and pay more attention to the moment.

Giving Birth Is Miraculous

By bringing children into the world, we have a heightened sense of connection and feel more deeply involved with humanity.

Giving birth is depicted by many women in what only can be described as sacred terms. We use language such as "miraculous," "awesome," and "wondrous" to try and capture the experience of creating a new life. By bringing children into the world, we have a heightened sense of connection and feel more deeply involved with humanity. Many of us are amazed by the emotions we feel in the presence of a newborn: love, protectiveness, hope, awe, responsibility, and gratitude. In her book *Growing with Your Child,* Elin Shoen describes the intense bond many mothers feel with their child, and also the connection they feel through their child to something much larger, to things more easily felt than explained.[57] Going through labor and delivery may awaken our interest in a spiritual practice as we try to find a framework in which to understand the miracle of birth.

We often speak with reverence of our children's births and our part in the creation process. Rosemary, now a mother of three, says, "I was awed by the miracle of birth. Even though it was miraculous to carry a baby for nine months and to feel the stirrings of life inside of me, there was something about the moment of birth and the moments after birth that were such pure joy. I never felt closer to God than I did each of the times I gave birth. It's such a profound experience. I feel that God is there at that moment of delivery. It's a testament to his presence. I think my husband felt it too. In some ways, it's even more dramatic because he didn't have the experience of nurturing a growing child inside him for nine months. So birth is quite dramatic. We were totally awed."

Our sense of continuity and connection may be heightened when our baby is born. Rebecca says, "Just after my daughter was born, I was lying in the hospital and all of a sudden I thought, 'I get it.' I understood life and death. I understand the cycle of life. Here's my little daughter who is an hour old named after her great-grandmother who is eighty-nine years old. They're both in diapers and neither of them can take care of themselves. I thought about how my daughter has a long life ahead of her and how I, as a mother, played such an important role in this continuing evolution of the human race."

Heather describes her daughter's birth as spiritually moving because she was completely free to be herself: "Giving birth was a spiritual experience for me because it was so miraculous and otherworldly. We went into the hospital on a Saturday night. It was eerily quiet. We were the only couple in the hospital. I was in labor from midnight until six in the morning, and as the sun came up and the birds started chirping, I gave birth. Literally I came out of the darkness with the arrival of my daughter. This all made it seem special and somehow divinely ordained. I gave birth naturally, which also added to the intensity, because I don't think I've ever felt as free to be me. I was absolutely 'me' in my purest form, both beautiful and ugly. I didn't have to be anything other than who I was or feel anything other than what I felt. I was the essence of who I am."

I Never Knew I Could Feel So Much Love

We learn to love and give in new ways.

Loving our child, we feel emotions that many of us have never felt before for another person. We love our baby without reservations or conditions. Elin Schoen writes, "For the first time, the new parent may experience a love that expects no rewards except the privilege of feeling this way. Many parents did not believe they had the potential for this kind of love — until it happened."[58] We learn to love and give in new ways. And sometimes we are amazed at how much our children love us back, despite our inexperience and imperfections as beginning parents.

For many of us the love we feel for our child is the best part of being a parent. Janet observes, "I'm totally nuts about my daughter, which has been one of the greatest things about parenting. For the first time in my life, I feel thoroughly close and intimate with another human being. I feel unconditional love for her in a way that I feel for nobody else. I don't even use the word 'love' to describe my relationship with anybody, sometimes not even my husband, because I don't come at it with this unfettered openness. With my husband, it's a partnership and I love him, but I'm crazy about my daughter."

Our capacity for unqualified love toward our children often amazes us. Joyce has two children ages three-and-a-half and one-and-a-half. She describes how selfless her love for her children is when she says, "The biggest impact for me has been realizing how much I love my children. I care more about them than I do about myself. I would do anything for my kids, and honestly there's no one else I would say that about, including my parents and siblings. I would kill first and think later with my children. That's a very powerful feeling. It's wonderful, but it's scary that there are people in your life that you feel that strongly about."

A mother of two small children and an ordained minister, Robin says that the most spiritual part of being a mother is the love she feels for her children. That absolute love has given her a greater understanding of a loving God. She says, "What children do is mirror the relationship that God has with us, if you think of us as God's children. I guess that's probably the biggest spiritual piece of it. We see how we are with our children, and we can only imagine how God feels about and deals with us. Also the notion of being willing to do anything for my child: I don't think we can understand that until we have a child of our own. It helps us understand that God would do whatever it took for us. Obviously it's a different proportion and level in terms of how God relates to us, but it gives me a small picture. All the stuff we experience as a parent, God experiences as God. There's a lot we can learn from that."

I'm Blessed

Our children make us appreciate our blessings, and in turn we
want to teach them how to notice the things in their lives for
which they can be thankful.

One of the overwhelming emotions we feel as new mothers is gratitude. We are thankful to have a healthy baby and to experience the wonder of parenthood. Our children make us appreciate our blessings, and in turn we want to teach them how to notice the things in their lives for which they can be thankful. Part of our gratitude comes from a heightened sense of vulnerability. We are more aware of our own frailties and of the fragility of life. Nancy Fuchs is an author, a mother, and a rabbi. She observes in her book *Our Share of Night, Our Share of Morning* that having children allows us to stop and focus on those aspects of our lives for which we feel thankful, even when things aren't going perfectly. She adds that creating rituals can help create a "habit of appreciation" in our family.[59]

Spiritual connection and gratitude seem to be intertwined for new mothers. Teresa says, "I thank God that my pregnancy went well and that our son was born healthy. When our son was a newborn, I would pray, 'Please don't let anything bad happen to him. Please don't let him suffer.' What I realize is that it's not by my own design that we were given this wonderful baby. He's healthy, happy, and delightful to be with. I feel very grateful for that."

Having a child may open up a greater sense of gratitude for all of life. Heather says, "I absolutely feel more gratitude now that I'm a mother. One of the things that we've started doing spontaneously is saying grace before our meals to remind ourselves how much we have to be thankful for. We don't address it to anyone in particular, but we say it to remind ourselves how fortunate we are relative to others. I also think showing thanks is a good thing to model for your child."

Spiritual fulfillment may come not only in our connection with our own children but with our extended family as well. At age thirty-five, Frances is a new mother who feels lucky to have twins. With two new babies she's had to rely on other people more than ever before and is thankful that her family has been there to help. She comments, "The spiritual aspect of parenting manifests itself in really basic ways. Having twins is such a special event. The odds of having spontaneous twins are so low (only 3 in 1,000) and for us to have had them makes me feel really lucky. The babies have provided an opportunity for my extended family to come together to celebrate. That's the biggest source of spiritual fulfillment for me."

Robin, the minister, defines a spiritual practice in terms of what is it that she pays attention to. She says, "One way to live a spiritual life is to come together in community and share in community what you are grateful for. With our kids, we simply sit down with them and ask, 'What were you most thankful for and least thankful for today?' Part of it is trying to cultivate that sense of spirit. What is it that you notice? Where was God? Where you are thankful for something, it's a gift from God. If you're not thankful, is there any way that God could have been in that for you? Obviously at their age, they're not going to get it entirely, but as they get older and think about it, that question will become part of their being. We're helping them notice spirit, notice how God is present in all circumstances. To me that's what the spiritual journey is about as a parent."

Caroline talks more to God now that she is a mother. She explains, "I feel thankful on a daily basis. When my first baby was born, I was so hormonal and appreciative; I was constantly saying prayers, mostly to keep my baby alive. Just the other day, I was driving somewhere with my kids in the car and we had a close call. I stopped the car and said, 'We've got to have a prayer.' I said, 'Thank you, God, for watching out for us and making me a cautious driver. Thank you for making me go slow and carefully even though we're late.' Then I got on a roll and said, 'I'm honored to be the mother of these people in the car. I know you expect great things from them, and I'm thankful to get to be their mom.' Sometimes my kids think I'm crazy, but I want to bring a sense of gratitude into our everyday life."

Motherhood Is More Fulfilling Than I Thought

Children, unlike work, remind us to enjoy the moment.

Being a mother can be a deeply satisfying experience. Although there are other paths to fulfillment, children give additional meaning and importance to our lives. Children require us to be fully engaged, and amidst the moments of frustration, there are moments of overwhelming joy. Many of us, especially older mothers, feel that we've waited a long time to have children, so we want to savor the experience. Or maybe our feelings of contentment as new mothers is simply a function of being so busy we don't have time to question our purpose in life. But ultimately, loving and caring for a child enhances and gives significance to our daily existence.

Though we may enjoy our work, often we find mothering

more emotionally satisfying. Virginia continues her consulting work on a reduced schedule and says that becoming a mother has been the most fulfilling thing she's done to date. She relates, "I was thirty-seven when my son was born, and I'd been through my 'the world is my oyster' episode. I felt good about where I was in my job. And from a personal perspective, I'd traveled a lot and had done a lot of interesting things. But motherhood has definitely been the most satisfying experience I've had so far, although I wouldn't be honest if I didn't say that it's also been the most challenging."

Children, unlike work, remind us to enjoy the moment. Julia is a working mother of two small children. She says, "Having children puts you in touch with experiencing the moment, seizing the day, really living, and being in touch with the joy of it. It's an amazing thing. For all these years, I've had great jobs but haven't had that much joy working. I'm fulfilled by my work, and I have good days and bad days. But it doesn't give me that feelings of total joy and fulfillment that I have playing in the grass at church or looking at a worm with my son."

Now an at-home mother of three, Beth says that being a mother is unquestionably fulfilling but also observes that fulfillment comes from a variety of sources. She relates, "Being a mother is fulfilling in a very nurturing and emotional kind of way. I find great joy in being around my kids and watching them grow. I love every little accomplishment from holding a spoon to tying a shoe. But for me, fulfillment comes in a lot of different ways that don't always involve kids. I'm very involved with my kids and I want them to grow up to be good people, but I don't get all my satisfaction from being a parent. Being appreciated for my other skills and intelligence are important for me too."

Sharon had her baby when she was thirty-eight years old and has stopped working to be at home with her daughter. She says, "Being a parent is a spiritual practice for me. I love being a mother. This is absolutely fulfilling, and I never would have imagined that I would feel this way. I'm in that category of woman who is leading a life right now that I never expected. This is so far and above anything I've ever done in terms of my spiritual fulfillment. I've spent a lot of time learning about Eastern religions, but I don't feel pulled to do that right now because my spiritual needs are being met. Hands down, I'm much more content on a daily basis than I've ever been. And that's what I was working toward before I became a mother: peace of mind. This feels right for me. I just know I'm supposed to be doing this, even though I'm not sure why yet."

Being a Mom Is the Hardest Thing I've Ever Done

*The responsibility of caring for another person inspires us to
find what is best in ourselves.*

If, in life, the situations that challenge us the most are the ones
from which we learn the most, then there's nothing quite like
having small children to show you who you really are. The
responsibility of caring for another person inspires us to find
what is best in ourselves. As mothers we may discover new
reserves of patience, wisdom, and compassion. At the same
time, being a mom brings out the worst in us more often than
we'd like to admit. What new mother hasn't been pushed to
her limit by an inconsolable newborn or a petulant two-year-
old? But when we can find the emotional resources to "act like
an adult" despite our own anger, frustration, and fear, we not
only set a good example for our children, we also grow as
individuals.

Having a child helps us discover ourselves. Donna has
learned a lot about herself being a mother. She says, "I've
always had motherly instincts, but they were deeply buried
until I had a child of my own. Having a baby has brought out
all sorts of new aspects of my personality. I'm a lot less self-
centered than I used to be. I find I am more patient with my
son than with anyone else in the world. In fact, my husband
thinks it's amazing how patient I am with our son and thinks

that maybe I should treat him more like I treat our little boy!"

Children challenge us to confront the parts of ourselves that we'd rather avoid. Grace finds it difficult to deal with feelings of anger toward her child. She says, "One of the hardest emotions for me as a parent is anger. Sometimes I get so mad at my daughter. I've tried it all: counting to ten, deep breathing, and trying to focus on the behavior instead of the child. When I do lose it, I try to apologize later. I just keep trying to stay focused on the fact that I'm dealing with another little soul who needs my love even when she's doing everything to drive it away. That can be hard."

Rachael has two children less than two years apart. She says, "I think the job of being a mother is the hardest thing I've ever done, and I worked for more than ten years in a very stressful environment before having kids. When I worked, if I was feeling bad, I could just sit at my desk and avoid everyone. But with two small children, you can't just ignore them when you don't feel up to dealing with them. I amaze myself sometimes that I'll feel so awful and yet I'm not awful to my kids. Usually I tap into some inner strength, and I rise to the occasion. So I might put on one more video than I normally would, but I'm still a good mom. I shock myself sometimes because I didn't know this compassion was there. But deep inside of me, there it is. I realize that I'm doing pretty well as a mother and I'm proud of that. I give myself a lot of credit for that."

I'm Learning to Give Up Some Control

Motherhood teaches us to be more flexible.

Many of us are humbled when we become mothers and realize that we aren't always in control. This can be a big shock for those of us who spent our pre-baby years believing that we had the power to direct the course of our lives. Right from the start, embarking on motherhood makes us aware of our limitations. We can't count on the timing of our pregnancy, the gender of our offspring, the temperament of our child, or the characteristics our children do and don't inherit from us. Motherhood teaches us to be more flexible. How can we expect to completely control our family life when we aren't even sure how a trip to the park will go on any given day? We find instead that we are always adapting to our children's changing moods, developmental stages, and personalities. In the end, we need to accept our children as they are without relinquishing our responsibility to guide them. And when faced with our own vulnerability, we see that it's okay to not have all the answers.

In letting go of control, we develop flexibility. A mother of two — a four-year-old and a two-year-old — Charlotte is learning to accept that she's not always in charge. She explains, "The biggest thing that motherhood has shown me is that I have to be incredibly flexible. With my first child, I would come up with these long lists of things I had to do and say to myself, 'This is what I have to accomplish today,' and I'd be really upset if I didn't achieve all my goals. I had to get over that. Now I don't get as uptight about being late or showing up with my kids in dirty clothes. I just swallow my pride and rejoice in getting somewhere at all. I've had to give up my image of always having a clean house or serving well-balanced meals. Sometimes my house is a mess and we eat dinner at McDonald's and you know what, it doesn't make any difference. I've just had to give up some control."

Our feelings of powerlessness may lead us to a new spiritual understanding. Eleanor says that mothering small children has pushed her to believe in a higher force. She says, "I'm a control freak and one of the things I've realized about having children is that I don't always have control. I think that's why I've turned to my faith more because I don't have control. I've had to resort to thinking, 'Okay, whatever will be will be. This is not for me to decide.'"

One of the gifts of motherhood is the freedom that comes with admitting that we don't know all the answers and that it's okay to ask for help. Marcia, a single mother, observes, "Motherhood is such a process of feeling your way through. You have to not be too hard on yourself when you make mistakes, because you're not going to do everything perfectly the first time. You have to go by your gut. When something isn't working, you do it differently. I've learned to be open to mothering in lots of different ways and to not have my heart set on being a certain kind of mother or having a certain kind of child. I've learned to get over my preconceived notions and to try something new. I've also learned to ask for help. I'm no longer afraid of doing that because everyone loves to give it, and I can always use it."

I'm More Compassionate

For some, the act of nurturing a small child allows us to nurture ourselves.

As mothers, children teach us about forgiveness. We accept our children because we love them and because we see how quick they are to forgive us. We may try to be less judgmental about others, because being a parent can bring our own weaknesses into relief. We realize that we are all trying to do the best we can and that as new mothers, each of us has had our lapses of patience and common sense. For some, the act of nurturing a small child allows us to nurture ourselves. In the process, we realize that we don't need to be a perfect mom to raise children who are secure and content.

For Lucy, her thirteen-month-old son has made her less negative and more appreciative of the wonder in life. She says, "What parenting has shown me is to practice more unconditional love and to watch my judgments. I know that my judgments are going to become my child's judgments. He's going to pick up on both the things I feel positive about and the things I feel negative about. So I've had to examine my own negativities and get rid of them. I think small children see beauty and perfection in everything. I don't want to spoil my son's sense of things being perfect with my adult biases."

The flip side of judgment is compassion. Sharon says, "Having a child has made me more aware of my natural tendencies to judge, and that's not how I want to be because I don't think there's one right way to be a parent. However, I'm doing what I think is right for my child, so I do have an opinion. One of the most challenging aspects of being a mother is redefining your relationships, especially with people you're friends with, so that you can be with someone without judgment when their parenting is so different from yours. It really calls for compassion. So being a parent has made me more aware of my judgment but also more compassionate toward other parents and toward other children."

Letting go of our images of perfection helps us connect with others. According to Cynthia, we have to be honest about ourselves and our children if we expect to get support from other mothers. She says, "One of the things I'm learning to do is to think and talk about children, mine and others, without judgment. That's been a complete evolution for me. Before I was a parent, I thought I knew a lot more than I did about child rearing. Now I realize just how little I do know. The less judgmental you are about your own parenting and about other people's parenting, the happier you'll be and the more you'll be able to be friends with other mothers. And that's important, because if you don't treat other mothers non-judgmentally, they'll be too scared to tell you what's really going on and then you won't have any support. You have to cop to the fact that things are not always perfect, so you can get some help from other mothers."

Having Children Allows Me to Live in the Moment

Children give us a chance to live in the world one moment at a time, so that even a trip to the corner mailbox becomes a nature hike when accompanied by a curious toddler.

Young children force us to slow down and rediscover the world. Their wonder and innocence make us feel young ourselves and put us more in touch with our physical environment. But stopping and appreciating the moment is not always easy for grown-ups to do. We adults go quickly about our business crossing tasks off our "to-do" lists. When we become mothers, we realize that being with children is not about what they do but who they are. Children give us a chance to live in the world one moment at a time, so that even a trip to the corner mailbox becomes a nature hike when accompanied by a curious toddler.

Cynthia's children have taught her be less task oriented and more open to the here and now. She says, "Having children allows you to focus on what's important. Before I was a mother, I was living life and being selfish and not really thinking about it too much. Now I see how important it is to live each day well and to set a good example. To me that means how I've treated people that day and whether I've fulfilled my responsibilities. I'm much less goal oriented. I'm glad of that because it allows me to enjoy the little things, to smell the roses so to speak. That's a real gift. In my former life, I was always trying to attain a goal, to get somewhere, to accomplish things. With children, there's such joy in the little things, like when your baby smiles or takes her first steps."

One of the wonderful things about children is how expressive they are. Grace marvels at how quickly a child's moods change: "I've been amazed by how quickly the emotions come and go with small children. One minute the world is going to end because their toast isn't cut in the right shape, and the next minute they're giggling about something they found in their pants pocket. I love the way they don't hold a grudge. That's something my daughter is teaching me: to get through my emotions and move on to the next one."

Audrey discusses the pleasure we experience when we see the world through our young children's eyes. She says, "There's a part of me that wants to believe in miracles. I think, 'Maybe I should just take a shot and believe that there's more going on than I can verify.' I want to weave some of that magic into the rest of my life. I don't want to be consumed by it, but I do want to keep alive my ability to feel it. Kids really help you do that."

My Faith Has Deepened As a Parent

*We want to make sure that our home life is consistent with
what we're saying.*

Many of us are looking for a framework in which to explore
the spiritual aspects of motherhood. For some, giving birth is
the event that brings us more in touch with matters of faith.
For others, it's the day-to-day lessons that being a new mother
teaches us or our sense that we are responsible for our children's spiritual sustenance as well as their physical well-being.
Although we may go to church "for our children," we often
find that there's something there for us as well. For many, it's
a community of faith, which provides our families with a
refuge in an unpredictable world.

For those of us who had a strong religious identity before
becoming mothers, having children can deepen our faith.
Introducing our beliefs and practices to our children is an
important part of expressing who we are. Many of us feel a
responsibility to pass on the faith and traditions that our parents gave us. We believe that children are spiritual by nature
and want to foster their sense of the miraculous. Being part of
a religious community can make us feel like we belong and
that there are others who share our beliefs and values. We
worship in a congregation of people to show our children that
there are other people who believe what we believe and live
by the same moral code.

Before she was married, Sally and her husband were committed Christians. Their commitment hasn't changed, but as a parent of a three-year-old and a one-year-old, they emphasize different things in their religious life. She says, "Now I focus on my children's religious education. I focus on our home life. We want to make sure that our home life is consistent with what we're saying. We want to act the way we talk. It makes us very conscious of what we say at home, what we say to each other. It's fun for me to help introduce them to their faith. With kids, it's mostly a different emphasis. Before we had kids, we were leaders in our church group. We decided we wanted to get out of our leadership role and just do something that would put us with our kids. We've been trying to figure out how to incorporate 'mission' into our daily life. Our kids should be able to look at my husband and me and say that our faith is real because we act it out."

Some of us believe that religious observance and identity are important values to instill in and communicate to our children. Joan describes her family as more observant than most families she knows. She believes that it's important to her to raise her three children with a strong Jewish identity. She says, "The most important reason is for my kids to feel like they are part of a community of people who do the same things and act in the same ways for the same reasons that we do. Plus it's important for children to have a belief set about God and things greater than they are. I think it's hard to raise kids without a set of rules that you follow because that's what's right.

They don't do things only because their parents say so, but because the Bible says we do. Children need to have a place where they can experience wonder and awe and a higher belief system. I want them to have rituals and a sense of something living on."

Yet, even as we are nurturing the spiritual lives of our children, it can be difficult to foster our own. Joan goes on to say how hard it is to pursue a spiritual practice when you are the mother of three small children: "I have to say that going to services and holiday celebrations at the synagogue is not always meaningful to me right now. There are very few times that I feel spiritually moved in synagogue, because so much of the time I can't focus on what's going on. When it's time to pray, one of my kids needs to go to the bathroom or they're whispering back and forth and bothering the other people. So most of the things that provide spiritual meaning for me take place in our home. Judaism is a very home-centered religion anyway. We've made a conscious decision to observe the Sabbath every week. We light candles and have a special dinner and spend time together as a family. My kids know that on Friday nights we'll be together at home. For us, it's about setting aside time and sanctifying it."

Through observances of our faith, we encourage our children's innate spirituality. Rosemary describes herself as growing up in a religious family that went to church every Sunday. She says, "I think it's important to raise children with a religious identity because children are naturally spiritual beings and come to questions of 'Who am I?' on their own. They have a deep hunger to understand where they came from and why they are here. I wanted them to have a sense of an overall guiding purpose of life. My faith is part of who I am and I want my children to share it. Whether they accept it or not will be their decision, although I hope they do accept it. I feel that I have a responsibility to teach my children what I was taught. I wouldn't be true to myself if I didn't teach them what I believe."

Rosemary concludes by observing that she started going to church again regularly because of her children, but found that it was addressing many of her own needs. She says, "Part of having a child is the recognition of your own mortality, because your children are the next generation who will succeed you. I think about death and the cycle of life. I started out thinking I would take my children to church for their religious education, but found that going to church dovetailed with my own needs to deal with my own life purpose and, ultimately, my own mortality. It comes down to how you want to conduct your own life. What kind of person are you? What's your purpose in life? So I've found that going to church is helping me address issues that are coming up anyway now that I'm older and am responsible for shaping the moral character of my children."

I Feel Like I Need to Go to Church Again

When we become parents, some of us may wrestle with our
desire to provide moral and spiritual guidance to our children
and our discomfort with some religious doctrine.

Often the question of our religious beliefs and affiliation are unaddressed until we have children. Although we describe ourselves as "religious" or "spiritual," many of us are still trying to figure out what we believe. When we become parents, some of us may wrestle with our desire to provide moral and spiritual guidance to our children and our discomfort with some religious doctrine. Unlike many in our parents' generation, we may not feel affiliated with one specific denomination. Many of us have investigated a variety of religious institutions in our quest for a community in which we feel comfortable. And those of us who are in interfaith couples may struggle to put together a practice of worship and set of family traditions that embody aspects of both of our religions. A 1993 study, cited in Phil Catalfo's book *Raising Spiritual Children in a Material World,* found that two-thirds of the baby boomers who went to church or synagogue as children stopped going as young adults, yet half of these people returned to religion, primarily because they had become parents.[60]

Even when we have our own doubts, we may feel it important for our children to join in religious rituals. Gina talks about the importance of raising her daughter in a church even though she has reservations about organized religion: "My husband is Catholic and I'm Episcopalian, but we go to an Episcopal church that we both like. I believe it's important for my daughter to have the ritual. I'll be conflicted about the substance later, but I want her to be exposed to it. I think just as long as there's a spiritual existence, it's not as important to me what church it is — as long as we feel comfortable there."

As a mother, Grace returned to the church at age thirty-eight and discusses how her religious upbringing made an impact on her even though she hadn't gone to church in twenty years: "I grew up going to church every Sunday but stopped when I went to college. Part of it was that as a child and teenager, I didn't think I was getting a lot out of it. I thought it was boring. In retrospect, I see that I learned some fundamental lessons that are a big part of who I am and what I value as an adult. Now that I have a daughter of my own, I've started going to church again because I think it's important for her to be raised as 'something.' She may reject it later on, but at least I'm giving her something to rebel against. I think it's important to have a religious foundation so she can take comfort in there being more to life than meets the eye — and frankly, I need that too."

I'm Still Seeking

*Children are intuitively more in touch with spiritual matters,
and that can make us more mindful of these issues.*

Many of us aren't sure that being part of an organized place of worship is necessary for our spiritual life. In the study mentioned earlier, 28 percent of the baby boomers who responded described themselves as "religious" or "spiritual" without being part of a specific denomination.[61] In other words, many of us are pursuing an individualized approach to meeting our spiritual needs. And in fact, in the same study 80 percent of the people who were interviewed felt that you could be a good Christian without going to church.[62] We view ourselves as spiritual people but are not always at ease with organized religion. We believe we can express our sense of values and morals through intention and example. Our hope is to demonstrate the importance of spirituality to our children and to nourish their souls in ways that are meaningful for our families.

Though we may feel ambivalent about our own religious beliefs, we still wonder what we should do about our children's spiritual education. Frances has been a mother for four months. She says laughingly, "My husband and I are looking to each other to become the religious figurehead for our family. It's not a big issue for either of us, because religion wasn't a part of our independent lives or our lives as a couple. I get spiritual fulfillment elsewhere and would like to figure out how to bring that into our family life. This is an unresolved issue for us. I value the religious more as an educational experience. It gives you a touch point when dealing with other people, but beyond that I'm not willing to sign up for weekly rituals. I love family rituals, but my religious experience has never been a source of major fulfillment in my life. My husband feels the same way. The big question mark is what do we do with our kids."

Children are intuitively more in touch with spiritual matters, and that can make us more mindful of these issues. Cynthia says, "I love being a mother. I feel connected to a whole in bringing a life into the world. My grandfather died when my oldest daughter was two. I was just barely pregnant with my second child, although my first wouldn't have known that I was pregnant yet. We were driving in the car and I was very sad. My daughter asked, 'Are you sad because Grandpa is dead?' And I replied that I was sad for me and sad for my grandmother that he was gone. And she said to me, 'Don't worry, Mommy. He'll come back as a baby.' I almost drove off the road. Here I was pregnant with my second baby and she said this unprovoked. I don't believe in reincarnation or God per se and I'm very up in the air about my beliefs in general, but that really gave me pause."

Cynthia continues by saying that there are other ways to teach values rather than by going to a church or synagogue: "I was taught values within my family. I have a very strong moral sense and that's where I will teach my children values. I think you teach by example. I see other people going to church when they become parents, but I couldn't do that. It would be hypocritical of me."

In our busy lives, church can seem like it interferes with family time. Eve grew up in a Jewish family, but is reluctant to send her children to Sunday school because Sunday is one of the few days her family can be together in an unhurried way. She says, "I have strong reservations about sending my children to Sunday school because, from a selfish perspective, I'd rather we did things together like going and playing in the park. So I have to figure out what's important about the tradition and what I want to impart. From my own upbringing, I went to Sunday school but I didn't feel like it provided a moral framework or values. Anything that shaped my worldview came from my family rather than from my religion. I certainly identify with being Jewish, but I don't think it has to do with the content of the religion; it's more of a social, cultural thing. And I don't think my religion provided me with any sense of spirituality. If I had any sense of spirituality it came from somewhere else. So I'm ambivalent about how to provide that for my own children."

Interfaith couples face the challenge of how to express their faith in a unified way. For Victoria and her husband it is difficult to agree on a church to attend together, and yet being together as a family is an important part of a spiritual practice for her. She says, "My husband and I are different religions. I went to church regularly as child but moved away from it as a teenager and in my twenties. When we had kids, I wanted to bring it back into our family but we couldn't decide on a church. So I took my daughter to my church. But it seemed awkward because Sunday was the one day we could be together as a family, and we were spending half the day apart. I didn't feel right about it because the whole family wasn't there, and having the family together was one of the values I wanted to promote. We talked about going to some other place, but we still haven't done it. I believe that values are taught at home, so I don't want to use the church as a crutch. Going to church is a good way to learn about religion and that's a good experience for a child, but I don't believe at a spiritual level that I'm not going to go to heaven because I don't go to church. We're still thinking about these issues."

We Want to Celebrate Our Baby's Birth

Celebrations of birth can be a time to bring our families and friends together and to make a public commitment to nurture our child's spiritual life.

As parents, we are responsible for our children's moral education as well as their physical care. Celebrations of birth can be a time to bring our families and friends together and to make a public commitment to nurture our child's spiritual life.

Many of us think it is important to baptize our babies or to perform a bris or naming ceremony to commemorate their birth. Some of us may even create our own ceremonies. These celebrations may draw upon a variety of traditions from our familial and cultural heritage as well as our religious upbringing. The questions of how we want to live and what we believe that are raised in our celebrations of birth will be part of an ongoing spiritual journey for parents and children.

Our sense of the spiritual may combine traditional and natural expressions. Rebecca discusses her daughter's baptism: "I think it's important to have certain values and morals reinforced through church going. I developed my own sense of spirituality, but I think it's a result of the foundation my parents provided by taking us to church. We baptized my daughter in the gown that my great-great-grandfather had worn. On the day we baptized her, it was pouring rain. We went to the church in the rain and it was perfect, because our sense of God is based partly in nature and the outdoors. It seemed so fitting that she was baptized by the rain, the same day she was baptized with holy water by the priest."

As we have more children, our celebrations of their births may evolve. The mother of three, Joan had Jewish celebrations for the births of each of her children. She recalls, "With our first daughter, we did a naming ceremony and it was very perfunctory. I don't remember feeling invested. I just felt like it had to be done. I did it for our families, because I wanted my daughter to be connected to them and to a religious tradition. With our second child, a boy, we did a bris, with a circumcision and a naming ceremony. Because of the circumcision, I thought about what it meant a lot more. I didn't feel particularly joyful about causing him that pain, but it had a lot more religious significance. With our third child, a daughter, we made a big deal out of the naming ceremony because we didn't want her to get shortchanged. We didn't use the traditional service but wrote our own ceremony, which we borrowed from a lot of different sources. It felt more meaningful to have done it that way."

Stephanie is a lesbian mother who left the congregation in which she was raised because she felt that it was not a hospitable environment for her. Her partner is taking the lead on her two-year-old son's religious education. She observes, "I don't know that I myself could make the commitment to having religion be a regularized part of our son's upbringing. However, we did a naming ceremony when he was three months old. It was an incredibly moving, emotional, wonderful experience. I'm touched by the power of a religious congregation brought together in a sense of love and tolerance and acceptance, which this congregations was, the power that that has to touch you deeply. I really appreciate that and I want him to have those experiences."

Creating our own celebrations may be more meaningful for us. Audrey was raised Catholic and her husband is Jewish. When their son was born, they designed their own ceremony to celebrate the birth. She recalls, "In our talking about what we wanted to do, we decided that the ceremony should be a blessing for the baby but also for the mother in recognition of what she had done. So my husband planned it all. He thought it was important that he plan it so that it would truly feel like a party for me too. We talked about what we wanted to do — readings, songs, who would do which parts, and so on — then my husband wrote the whole thing. Many of our friends and families were invited. It was the first gathering of our son's community and really the first time since our wedding that we brought that cast of characters together. It was great. It was very heartfelt because it wasn't done by rote."

Audrey continues by discussing the difficulties of combining different religions and cultures: "I think the preparation for the event was a spiritual experience. Thinking and talking about what was important and what we wanted to communicate was great. The actual doing of the event was in some ways anticlimactic. It was more like a performance, so there was some anxiety associated with that. And because we gathered people from different backgrounds, we didn't know whether they were all on the same page. We're were dealing with the unspoken religious battlefield. It's hard to do something different and have it be meaningful to everyone."

I'm Enjoying the Holidays More

Celebrating the holidays helps us solidify our own sense of "family."

Many of us find that once we become parents, holidays become more important — and decidedly more festive. To see the traditions and rituals through the eyes of a child allows us to experience them anew. And very small children can appreciate the sights, smells, and sounds of holiday celebrations, even if they don't understand the religious or cultural significance of the event. As Elizabeth Berg writes in *Family Traditions*, "Celebrating lifts days away from other days. It gives us something to look forward to and makes a formal statement that life is full of things to be grateful for."[63] Whether we inherit them or create them, holiday celebrations remind us what's important in the midst of the day-to-dayness of parenting.

Some of us may choose to carry on the traditions of the family in which we grew up. Rosemary describes her holiday celebrations as "family based." She says, "We celebrate the way my parents did with us when we were children. We celebrate all the holidays, usually with relatives, although we don't live near most of them, so it's different relatives each year. My mother made a big deal of the holidays and so I remember them fondly. Now it's my turn to do that for my children."

Celebrating the holidays helps us solidify our own sense of "family." A mother of two, Joyce talks about how, around the holidays, she and her husband started to view themselves as their own family: "Yes we're part of our larger families, but we've really made a conscious effort to have our holidays in our home and not travel to either my family's or his family's for Christmas. We feel really strongly about that and have made it clear to our families, and everyone has accepted that. That's very important to us because we're our family now. We don't have to celebrate Christmas Day with our extended families anymore. It's nice to just say it and believe and feel it and practice it."

Sometimes we don't quite know how to celebrate the holidays because our family traditions and beliefs may differ from those of our partner. Doreen says she's still trying to figure out what her family's spiritual practice and holiday celebrations will look like. A mother of three, she says, "My husband's background is Jewish and my background is agnostic. His family wasn't very religious, so it was never a problem for the two of us because our values were so similar. But since the kids came along, it's been much harder. We celebrate both Hanukkah and Christmas. This year I learned a lot more about Hanukkah and discovered that one important aspect of Hanukkah is standing up for what you believe in. I had to ask myself, 'What do we believe in? How are we going to convey and demonstrate those beliefs to our children?' I know from my own childhood that a parent needs to practice what he or she preaches. So I can see that my husband and I are going to have to talk a lot more about this, because if we don't get it straight, we can't possibly demonstrate it or communicate it or live it with our children."

The holiday spirit can touch even the smallest child. A mother of four, Caroline says, "I think even little children can take in the spirit of the holidays. They smell the cookies baking and see the candles being lit. They appreciate the preparations and hopefully don't pick up on the stress of last-minute gift buying or feeling like you spent too much money. I think the challenge is to reduce the holidays to the rituals that reinforce your values."

It's Important to Start Family Traditions

Family traditions allow us to stop and cherish the moment and to feel that we are part of something bigger.

Traditions give us a sense of identity and belonging. They connect us with our extended families and communities and can make us more aware of our background, culture, and religious practices. Family traditions allow us to stop and cherish the moment and to feel that we are part of something bigger. And any parent knows that young children embrace routine. The ritualization of even small events brings a sense of predictability, security, and comfort — for children and parents alike. As Elizabeth Berg writes, "Traditions routinely put love, comfort and meaning into our lives . . . . A tradition doesn't have to be heavy and rigid. It can be something you do once and it feels right so you do it again."[64]

It is important to make the ordinary things special for both children and adults. Deborah appreciates how her parents did this for her, and she wants to do the same for her two-year-old son. She says, "Traditions don't have to be big things, but children remember them as the fabric of family. It creates some history and sense of permanence. That's a really big deal. My sister, who has a little girl, lives near me but we don't see each other very much. We've started to see each other more because we both want our children to have each other. I had them over around Easter so the kids could dye eggs together, which is something we did as a family growing up. It was fun to take that warm memory for both my sister and me and pass it down to our children."

Each family creates traditions that are singularly theirs. A mother of three, Rosemary says there are things that she and her family do regularly that are unique to their family: "There are certain things that we do every year. We go on vacation every summer in the same place. We attend opening day of the football season together. We pick apples every fall, and almost every Sunday night we go to the same restaurant for supper. It's important to have family traditions, to celebrate together, to have fun together and have certain things that we all enjoy doing together. I think doing things consistently year to year that are unique to your family defines and reinforces your sense of family."

Alicia recounts the Jewish traditions she and her husband have started celebrating with their two-and-a-half-year-old daughter: "Our traditions have a deeper religious component because there's more reason to do them now. There's a Jewish ceremony in the spring where you plant a new tree and say a little blessing. We did that with my daughter this year. Maybe we would have done it otherwise, but there's something about doing it with a child that gives it more significance. Every year we can show her that little tree and say to her, 'Remember when we did that?' Maybe we'll do it every year and have a line of trees. So it's not just religious traditions but all sorts of ritual that we're doing more now. I didn't have as much reason to do those things before we had a child. I just love all that stuff, anything that gives our lives meaning."

To give birth to and raise children is to embark on a spiritual path because children enhance our life and amplify its meaning. Whether we take this journey in an organized faith or through an individual quest, we find that there is nothing like motherhood to teach us poignant lessons about life. Who we are, what we believe, what we notice, and what we teach are all part of practicing spirituality with our families. Through parenting a baby or young children, we reach new levels of self-knowledge, wisdom, faith, and, most of all, hope.

NINE

I Have to Work at Creating Community

*The most profound feelings
come from being connected to
another human being. People
who are involved with others
live longer.*

— *Allan Luks*

Out of the strength of your community, you will be able to do things you never thought you were capable of.
— M. Scott Peck

One of the realities of modern American life is the loss of community that many of us feel. Although as a nation we have a long and admirable history of self-determination, the downside of individual freedom is that we don't always feel connected to a community of people. It's hard to feel a sense of cohesion in a culture where approximately 30 percent of us change addresses every two years.[65] This is not to say we don't have important people in our lives. Before having a baby, our workplace and professional associations made up an important community for us. Yet when we become mothers, our longing for a community beyond work becomes more acute, not only for practical support, but for our emotional and spiritual well-being.

We, who have always relished our mobility and independence, find ourselves reminiscing about the tight-knit communities of previous generations and the support and social ties they offered to new parents. Yet in their book on community making, Carolyn Shaffer and Kristin Anundsen write that our goal shouldn't be to try and re-create the past. Many of these earlier communities were based on obligation and a need for conformity. Today we have the opportunity to build our communities on a foundation of shared values and a sense of responsibility to one another.[66] In fact in their book on community organizing, George Bager, Harry Specht, and James Torczyner describe how "communities come into being to fulfill a specific purpose that its members cannot accomplish alone."[67] Surely parenthood falls into this category.

Belonging to a community fills our need for intimacy and combats some of the isolation and loneliness we may feel when we become new mothers. In his book *A Different Drum,* M. Scott Peck observes that in a true community, we feel accepted, appreciated, and heard. Yet he acknowledges that building community takes a lot of work. It requires an intention to communicate honestly, a willingness to accept differences among the members of the group, and a commitment to participate.[68] In return, we receive the gifts of security, identity, and belonging. Both adults and children benefit from knowing that there is an extended network of people who care about them and on whom they can depend, while still remaining true to themselves.

I Have Something in Common with All Mothers

At the most obvious level, many new mothers feel connected to other women for the simple reason that they are also mothers.

As Shaffer and Anundsen write, the word "community" has

been overused to describe a wide variety of affiliations and associations. While communities may exist as a function of circumstances or because of a conscious choices.[69] new mothers experience both. At the most obvious level, many new mothers feel connected to other women for the simple reason that they are also mothers. Whereas our post-college years were devoted to developing our independence and mastery of the world, we feel more a part of humanity when living in the world with children. We are more open and compassionate, and not as self-absorbed. Although not a community specific to a certain place or time, we share the universal experience of bringing babies into the world and rearing them. Often this new connection is made real through the kindness of people around us. True, there are times when the last thing we want is advice from a stranger about how to keep our baby warm when we're out on a walk. Yet on the whole, we are touched by the warmth and interest people show toward our new families.

Becoming a mother can open us up to other people. Veronica, a mother of two, says she started feeling connected to other mothers as soon as she became pregnant. She observes, "I think you start feeling connected when you become visibly pregnant. Other women will approach you and ask you questions and share their stories with you. As a mother, I feel connected to all life. How can you possibly not have empathy for anyone that's gone through the experience of having a baby? When I became a mom, my world became a little less myopic. I felt more connected to the universe."

Serena has a two-year-old and a new baby. She believes that being a parent gives you something in common with anyone else who is a parent. She says, "Everyone is so friendly when you have kids and it gives you a bond with them that you might not otherwise have. It's been interesting for me because my husband has all his grandparents so our kids have four living great-grandparents. His grandmothers were housewives all their lives so in some ways I didn't feel like I had a lot in common with them. But as a mother I now have this bond with them; we're all part of the club. Everyone has to potty train her children at some point, whether it was sixty years ago or today. All of a sudden you *do* have a lot in common."

I Need Other New Mothers

With other new moms, we can share information and resources while building confidence in our new role as a parent.

Although becoming a mother gives a sense of connection with other mothers, we don't automatically become friends with anyone who has a baby. We still have to take active steps to create a genuine community for our family. One of the most obvious places to start building a network is among other new mothers. Not only do they share our interests and concerns, they keep the same schedule. Through fellowship with other women, we gain insight as mothers and find humor in the ups and downs of parenting. With other new moms, we can share information and resources while building confidence in our new role as a parent. And it's only another mother who can truly commiserate when our toddler goes on a hunger strike. Whether it's through an organized mothers' group or an informal group of girlfriends, being around other moms provides us a unique place to share our questions, fears, and triumphs about life after baby.

Support groups with a specific focus can be invaluable. Heidi, a working mother, makes time to attend a group for new mothers of twins, sponsored by her local hospital. She values the wisdom of other women who share the specific experience of having multiples. She says, "I love this group. It's great because you can ask all those little questions that have been bothering you. Usually there is someone else in the group who has a child just your child's age or maybe someone who has a child six months older than yours who can give you some perspective. There was a woman there with triplets and she was describing her situation, and I thought, "I can never complain again." Attending those meetings really puts things in perspective for me."

The mother of a three-year old, Brenda meets regularly with a group of working moms. Once a month, they get together with their children and once a month, they gather without kids. She says, "I think the need for community is an underlying human drive. It's coded in our genes and comes forward when we become parents and it starts becoming more clear that we really need community. When my son was one, I started meeting with a group of working mothers. This group has been my lifeline. None of us have a lot of extra time, but it means our lives to get together. I feel that it's the only thing I do for myself, because *everything* else is done in the service of my job, my children, or my husband. In this group, we talk about everything. Sharing my experiences makes me realize that I'm not a bad mom and my child isn't abnormal. It's great because I can be less than a perfect mother and still be accepted by this group."

I'm More Involved in My Neighborhood

Of course, as a parent, I have more stake in the future because it's my child's future.

Sometimes, our sense of connectedness as a parent extends to our neighbors and manifests itself in an increased sense of civic responsibility. With children, we spend more time living and playing in our communities. We make an effort to get to know our neighbors and feel more responsible for our physical environment. Many of us find ourselves working in large and small ways to improve the neighborhoods and cities where we are raising our families.

Grace says that having children makes her more conscious of her neighborhood and the people who inhabit it.

She says, "When I walk down the street with my daughter, we move really slowly and say 'hi' to everyone along the way. I've had so many people do nice things for me — opening doors, helping with groceries — so I try to do more of that myself. That's where community starts — in the little gestures we make toward the people around us. As a mother, I know what it's like to struggle to do the basic things (like get in or out of a store door) and so I notice when other people are having a hard time and I help out more. Before I was a mother, I was moving too quickly to pay attention to other people. Having a baby has humanized my surroundings."

Our networks expand as our children get older. Alicia, the mother of a two-and-a-half-year-old, says, "Suddenly I realized that my daughter going school will involve her in knowing other children and our knowing the parents and needing to cooperate with them. This is partly the way we'll enter the community; having a child pushes us into it. I've started being active in the community. I'm part of a group that really wants to make our neighborhood a better place. Of course, as a parent, I have more stake in the future because it's my child's future. I have a more direct interest in traffic and safety issues, and the schools and playgrounds."

Alicia continues by discussing the drawbacks of interacting with a new group of people as well as the rewards of being active in a community: "It's very exciting to know people and be part of the community, but suddenly you're working with all these people! We're so involved and with that comes all the personalities. It can be frustrating sometimes, but I'm also really enjoying it. I think I would have been involved anyway, but having a child makes it more urgent and concrete. I have more reason to do this. This activism has been a good new thing in my life."

Can I Create Community on the Internet?

What the Internet offers many of us is an easy way to keep in touch.

Many of us feel that a sense of community only occurs when people are with each other face-to-face. Yet with 120 million Americans on-line[70], we are increasingly using the Internet to strengthen the ties that bind us. There's no question that an electronic message can never replace getting together for coffee with an old friend. However, the Internet can be a marvelous tool for mothers of babies and small children to stay connected with the world. The Internet can support new mothers by facilitating communication among our existing personal and professional networks. It can give us access to web sites that provide information, advice, and even products for parents. And it can introduce us to other new mothers.

What the Internet offers many of us is an easy way to keep in touch. One of the things that mothers of small children don't have is free time. Often we can't spare the half hour it takes to write a letter or make a telephone call. With e-mail, we don't have to spend a lot of time or money to connect with people. Instead, we can make contact from our home, without having to hire a baby-sitter or change out of our fuzzy slippers. E-mail gives us the flexibility to keep in touch when it's convenient for us (and while we can still remember our thought) rather than having to wait until a polite hour to call on the phone. This also holds true for making purchases on-line. Buying products on the Internet can be done from our computer, at any hour of the day or night, without the inevitable meltdown that occurs when we take a toddler with us on a shopping trip.

Casey has two children and finds that using the Internet allows her to do things on-line that would otherwise take time away from her family. She says, "As a nonworking mom, I view part of my job as creating community for my family. E-mail lets me communicate quickly with people, and I do a lot of buying on the Web. Basically I use the Internet to free up my time so I can spend more of it with my family and friends."

Electronic access to information can empower mothers and keep us connected to the larger world in ways that were impossible a few short years ago. Paula says, "I use the Internet when I want to learn about something. I often go to parenting web sites when I have a child-related question. Also, my father lives in another state and was recently diagnosed with an illness. I wanted to find out more about his condition so I went to the World Wide Web. I found medical information that enabled me to advocate for him from afar in a way I couldn't have done had I not had that information at my fingertips. Since mothers are usually the ones who are responsible for their family's health, it's really valuable to have access to such sophisticated knowledge. And finally, it's great to use the Web with kids. My four-year-old recently asked me about Martin Luther King. In my childhood, I went to the encyclopedia to look things up, but now I use the Internet. We not only found a picture of Dr. King, but discovered a web site that played parts of his speeches in his own voice. To a four-year-old, this was magic."

Although most new mothers don't have the time or inclination to make new friends on the Internet, there are some who have found supportive communities and developed genuine relationships on the Web. Shannon started spending time on the Internet when her son was a year and a half as a way to maintain adult interaction when she stopped working. She says, "When I left my job, I imagined myself becoming someone with a dust rag and a baby, who no one would want to know. I found an on-line community of mothers. There is limited access to this community, and everyone is required to use their real name, which makes people more responsible for their behavior. I exchange e-mails with these other women every day, so they know more about my day-to-day life than some of my other friends. We're more honest about what's really going on because we don't have to keep up appearances as much. I think virtual communities allow you to be more of who you are. I'm very sociable and this has allowed me to be more social and to get to know a broader spectrum of mothers. I've definitely expanded my community through the Internet."

I'm Building My Own Community

More than just shared interests, a genuine community offers love, support and the opportunity to learn about the range of human nature.

As career women, our primary community often revolved around our work. We made friends, shared experiences, and felt a sense of belonging in the professional world. One of the challenges of having a baby is realizing that our workplace may not provide the sustenance we need as parents and that we must look elsewhere for support in our new role as mothers. That said, the thought of creating our own communities can be daunting. Yet it can be as simple as getting a group of women together on a regular basis in the spirit of mutual support and assistance. Although it takes effort to create a community, we know it when we have it. More than just shared interests, a genuine community offers love, support, and the opportunity to learn about the range of human nature. And in a true community, we feel a sense of inclusion and acceptance that helps overcome some of the feelings of insecurity that may come with being a new mother.

Friendships among our mom friends can become so significant that these friends begin to seem like family. A mother of a three-year old and a one-year-old, AnnMarie talks about the friendships she's created among a remarkable group of women. She says, "Since I don't have family here, I've had to do a lot more outreach but it's really paid off. I feel so lucky because I have a wonderful group of friends who are mothers of small children. We look out for each other. They've gotten me through the hard times and the happy times of motherhood."

Our children bring people into our lives. Stephanie describes the network of friends who serve as an extended family to her two-year old son, and the role he's played in bringing this group together: "It's wonderful that our son has a community of people who care for him. And he has enriched the lives of our extended network of friends and that gets reflected back to him and his sense of self-esteem. He knows that there's a whole universe of people who want to be around him and who enjoy having him in their lives. It's not just that his two parents think he's the center of the universe and that he's terrific. Other people feel that way too. He's a gift to all of us."

Roberta, who moved across country when her son was three, has lived in her new hometown for six months. She shares this story about her developing community: "I'm often asked whether I've made new friends in my new home. Although friendships form slowly, I believe I can report progress. Jill and Karen and Jill's husband, Jeff, came to the hospital last night to make sure my son was okay after he fell off the back of the couch, hit his face, had a seizure, lost consciousness, and rode to the hospital in a 911 ambulance. Jill talked to the 911 guys and explained clearly what had happened. Leslie held my son and rocked him while I tracked down my husband. She waited for my husband to get home, told him how to get to the hospital, and closed up the house for us. Neighborhood kids ran down to the gate to make sure the emergency vehicles could get in and find the house. Karen lent us her car seat so we could get home. Jennifer and Ellen left messages saying, 'I heard that your son was hurt. Let me know if there is anything I can do.' And mostly, Jill and Karen were there."

Roberta concludes, "My son is fine. (The CT scan was a highlight for him: an elevator ride, a big machine going around and around, and a very cool computer to play with.) I am once again shattered by motherhood into 10,000 pieces and redeemed by the friendship and support of other women."

It would be wonderful if we lived in a culture where an existing network of relatives and friends mobilized when a baby was born to help take care of us and ease us into our new role as parents. More often than not, however, we have to build our own communities through intention and commitment. Yet when we find true communities, we discover that the sum of our individual talents is greater than the separate parts. As each member of the community contributes to the whole, we are rewarded with a role and a connection. May you build communities to support and sustain you throughout your adventures in motherhood.

Endnotes

ONE   Oh My Gosh, I Have a Baby!

[1] Anita Shreve, *Remaking Motherhood: How Working Mothers Are Shaping Our Children's Future* (New York: Viking, 1987), 16.

[2] Lucy Scott, Ph.D., and Meredith Joan Angwin, *Time Out for Motherhood: A Guide for Today's Working Women to the Financial, Emotional and Career Aspects of Having a Baby* (New York: St. Martin's Press, 1986), 102.

[3] M. S. Rosenthal, *The Fertility Sourcebook* (Los Angeles: Lowell House, 1995), 44.

[4] *The World Almanac and Book of Facts* (Mahwah, NJ: PRIMEDIA Reference, Inc., 1999), 745.

[5] T. Berry Brazelton, M.D., *Touchpoints: Your Child's Emotional and Behavioral Development* (Reading, MA: A Merloyd Lawrence Book/Perreus Books, 1992), 37–39.

[6] Marshall H. Klaus, M.D., John H. Kennell, M.D., and Phyllis H. Klaus, C.S.W., M.F.C.C., *Bonding: Building the Foundations of Secure Attachments and Independence* (Reading, MA: A Merloyd Lawrence Book/Addison Wesley, 1995), 45.

[7] *Ibid.*, 59.

[8] Arlene Eisenberg, Heidi E. Murkoff, and Sandee E. Hathaway, B.S.N., *What to Expect When You're Expecting* (New York: Workman Publishing Company, Inc., 1996), 383.

[9] Andrea Boroff Eagan, *The Newborn Mother: Stages of Her Growth* (Boston: Little, Brown and Company, 1988), 27.

[10] Brazelton, *Touchpoints*, 39–40.

[11] Eagan, *The Newborn Mother*, 27–28.

[12] U.S. Bureau of the Census, *Statistical Abstract of the United States: 1998, 118th edition* (Washington, DC: U.S. Government Printing Office, 1998), 89.

[13] Eagan, *The Newborn Mother,* 37.

[14] *Ibid.*

[15] Eisenberg, Murkoff, and Hathaway, *What to Expect,* 545.

[16] Eagan, *The Newborn Mother,* 43.

[17] Ted Ayllon, Ph.D., *Stopping Baby's Colic* (New York: A Perigree Book, 1989), 23.

[18] Sally Placksin, *Mothering the New Mother* (New York: Newmarket Press, 1994), 76.

TWO   I'm Not Sure How to Be a Mom

[19] Erik Erikson, *Identity and the Life Cycle* (New York: W. W. Norton, 1980), 103, 125.

[20] Andrea Boroff Eagan, *The Newborn Mother: Stages of Her Growth* (Boston: Little, Brown and Co., 1985), 39–150.

[21] Lucy Scott, Ph.D., and Meredith Joan Angwin, *Time Out for Motherhood: A Guide for Today's Working Women in the Financial, Emotional and Career Aspects of Having a Baby* (New York: St. Martin's Press, 1986), 100.

THREE   How Do I Integrate My Professional Self with Motherhood?

[22] U.S. Bureau of Census, *Statistical Abstract of the United States: 1999, 119th edition* (Washington DC: U.S. Government Printing Office, 1999), 413.

[23] Arlie Hochschild, *The Second Shift: Working Parents and the Revolution at Home* (New York: Viking, 1989), 272.

[24] Carolyn Pape Cowan and Philip A. Cowan, *When Partners Become Parents: The Big Life Changes for Couples* (New York: BasicBooks/HarperCollins, 1992), 121.

[25] Hochschild, *The Second Shift,* 7.

[26] Alison Clarke-Stewart, *Daycare* (Cambridge, MA: Harvard University Press, 1993), 7.

[27] Grace K. Baruch, Rosalind Barnett, and Caryl Rivers, *Lifeprints* (New

York: Prime Printing, 1983), 163.

[28] Bonnie Michaels and Elizabeth McCarty, *Solving the Work/Family Puzzle* (Business One Irwin, 1992), 39–40.

[29] Luisa Kroll, "Entrepreneur Moms," *Forbes,* 18 May, 1998, 84.

FOUR   Having a Baby Has Changed My Relationship with My Husband

[30] Jay Belsky and John Kelly, *The Transition to Parenthood: How a First Child Changes a Marriage* (New York: Delacorte Press, 1994), 29.

[31] *Ibid.*, 28–31.

[32] *Ibid.*, 33.

[33] *Ibid,* 40.

[34] Carolyn Pape Cowan and Philip A. Cowan, *When Partners Become Parents: the Big Life Change for Couples* (New York: BasicBooks/Harper Collins, 1992), 188–89.

[35] *Ibid.*, 12.

[36] *Ibid.*, 7.

FIVE   How Will Our Parents Be Involved with Our New Family?

[37] Arthur Kornhaber, *Between Parents and Grandparents* (New York: St. Martin's Press, 1986), 12–13.

SIX   How Do We Mother Daughters and Sons?

[38] Evelyn Bassoff, Ph.D., *Between Mothers and Sons: The Making of Vital and Loving Men* (New York: A Dutton Book/The Penguin Group, 1994), 65.

[39] Michael Gurian, *The Wonder of Boys* (New York: G. P. Putnam & Sons, 1996), 13.

[40] Jeanne Elium and Don Elium, *Raising a Daughter: Parents and the Awakening of a Healthy Woman* (Berkeley, CA: Celestial Arts, 1994), 14.

[41] Gurian, *The Wonder of Boys*, 16.

[42] Elium and Elium, *Raising a Daughter*, 19.

[43] Gurian, *The Wonder of Boys*, 5, 8.

[44] *Ibid.*, 6.

[45] Bassoff, *Between Mothers and Sons*, 17.

[46] *Ibid.*, 14.

[47] Elium and Elium, *Raising A Daughter*, 50, 59.

[48] Bassoff, *Between Mothers and Sons*, 52.

[49] *Ibid.*, 3.

[50] *Ibid.*, 52.

[51] *Ibid.*, 25.

SEVEN   We're Ready to Have More Children, Aren't We?

[52] Judy Dunn, *From One Child to Two* (New York: Fawcett Columbine, 1995), 4.

[53] Carla Harkness, *The Infertility Book: A Comprehensive Medical and Emotional Guide* (Berkeley, CA: Celestial Arts Publishing, 1992), 77.

[54] Harriet Fishman Simons, *Wanting Another Child: Coping with Secondary Infertility* (New York: Lexington Books, 1995), 4.

[55] Ellie McGrath, *My One and Only* (New York: William Morrow, 1989), 30.

[56] *Ibid.*

EIGHT   Motherhood Is a Spiritual Journey

[57] Elin Schoen, *Growing with Your Child: Reflections on Parental Development* (New York: Doubleday, 1995), 38.

[58] *Ibid.*, 42.

[59] Nancy Fuchs, *Our Share of Night, Our Share of Morning: Parenting As a Spiritual Journey* (San Francisco: Harper San Francisco/Harper Collins Publishers, 1996), 100.

[60] Phil Catalfo, *Raising Spiritual Children in a Material World* (New York: Berkley Books, 1997), 39.

[61] *Ibid.*

[62] *Ibid.*

[63] Elizabeth Berg, *Family Traditions: Celebrations for Holidays and Everyday* (Pleasantville, NY: Reader's Digest Association, 1992), 9.

[64] *Ibid.*, 9, 19.

NINE   I Have to Work at Creating Community

[65] Carolyn R. Shaffer and Kristin Anundsen, *Creating Community Anywhere* (New York: Jeremy P. Tarcher/Perigee Books, 1993), 4.

[66] *Ibid.*, 5–8.

[67] George Brager, Harry Specht, and James L. Torczyner, *Community Organizing* (New York: Columbia University Press, 1987), 36.

[68] M. Scott Peck, *The Different Drum: Community-Making and Peace* (New York: Simon and Schuster, 1987), 61–76.

[69] Shaffer and Anundsen, *Creating Community*, 9–12.

[70] Reuters: Gender Gap Has Almost Disappeared in U.S., Jan. 25, 2000. (www.nua.ie/surveys/index.cgi&f=VS&art_id=905355546&rel=true)

About the Author

Wynn McClenahan Burkett is a graduate of Stanford University and Yale School of Management. Following a career in investment banking and government, she now lives in San Francisco where she and her husband are raising two children.

About the Press

Wildcat Canyon Press publishes books that embrace such subjects as friendship, spirituality, women's issues, and home and family, all with a focus on self-help and personal growth. Great care is taken to create books that inspire reflection and improve the quality of our lives. Our books invite sharing and are frequently given as gifts.

For a catalog of our publications, please write:

Wildcat Canyon Press

2716 Ninth Street

Berkeley, California 94710

Phone: (510) 848-3600

Fax: (510) 848-1326

info@wildcatcanyon.com

or see our web site at www.wildcatcanyon.com

MORE WILDCAT CANYON TITLES...

STEPMOTHERS & STEPDAUGHTERS: RELATIONSHIPS OF CHANCE, FRIENDSHIPS FOR A LIFETIME
True stories and commentary that look at the relationship between stepmother and stepdaughter as strong, loving, and a life-long union.
Karen L. Annarino
$14.95 ISBN 1-885171-46-3

BOUNTIFUL WOMEN: LARGE WOMEN'S SECRETS FOR LIVING THE LIFE THEY DESIRE
The definitive book for women who believe that "bountiful" is a way of being in this world, not a particular size.
Bonnie Bernell
$14.95 ISBN 1-885171-47-1

AND WHAT DO YOU DO? WHEN WOMEN CHOOSE TO STAY HOME
At last, a book for the 7.72 million women who don't work outside the home—by choice!.
Loretta Kaufman and Mary Quigley
$14.95 ISBN 1-885171-40-4

40 OVER 40: 40 THINGS EVERY WOMAN OVER 40 NEEDS TO KNOW ABOUT GETTING DRESSED
An image consultant shows women over forty how to love what they wear and wear what they love.
Brenda Kinsel
$16.95 ISBN 1-885171-42-0

GUESS WHO'S COMING TO DINNER: CELEBRATING CROSS-CULTURAL, INTERFAITH, AND INTERRACIAL RELATIONSHIPS

True-life tales of the deep bonds that diversity makes.
Brenda Lane Richardson
$13.95 ISBN 1-885171-41-2

OUT OF THE BLUE: ONE WOMAN'S STORY OF STROKE, LOVE, AND SURVIVAL
A must read for stroke survivors and their families.
Bonnie Sherr Klein
$14.95 ISBN 1-885171-45-5

STILL FRIENDS: LIVING HAPPILY EVER AFTER...EVEN IF YOUR MARRIAGE
FALLS APART
True stories of couples who have managed to keep their friendships
intact after splitting up.
Barbara Quick
$12.95 ISBN 1-885171-36-6

CALLING TEXAS HOME: A LIVELY LOOK AT WHAT IT MEANS TO BE A TEXAN
Bursting with fascinating trivia, first-person accounts of frontier days,
curiosities, and legends of the people of Texas.
Wells Teague
$14.95 ISBN 1-885171-38-4

CALLING CALIFORNIA HOME: A LIVELY LOOK AT WHAT IT MEANS TO BE A
CALIFORNIAN
A cornucopia of facts and trivia about Californians and the California
Spirit.
Heather Waite
$14.95 ISBN 1-885171-37-4

CALLING THE MIDWEST HOME: A LIVELY LOOK AT THE ORIGINS, ATTITUDES,
QUIRKS, AND CURIOSITIES OF AMERICA'S HEARTLANDERS
A loving look at the people who call the Midwest home—whether they
live there or not.
Carolyn Lieberg
$14.95 ISBN 1-885171-12-9

BREASTS: OUR MOST PUBLIC PRIVATE PARTS
One hundred and one women reveal the naked truth about breasts.
Meema Spadola
$13.95 ISBN 1-885171-27-7

I WAS MY MOTHER'S BRIDESMAID: YOUNG ADULTS TALK ABOUT THRIVING IN
A BLENDED FAMILY
The truth about growing up in a "combined family."
Erica Carlisle and Vanessa Carlisle
$13.95 ISBN 1-885171-34-X

THE COURAGE TO BE A STEPMOM: FINDING YOUR PLACE WITHOUT LOSING
YOURSELF
Hands-on advice and emotional support for stepmothers.
Sue Patton Thoele
$14.95 ISBN 1-885171-28-5

CELEBRATING FAMILY: OUR LIFELONG BONDS WITH PARENTS AND SIBLINGS
True stories about how baby boomers have recognized the flaws of
their families and come to love them as they are.
Lisa Braver Moss
$13.95 ISBN 1-885171-30-7

AUNTIES: OUR OLDER, COOLER, WISER FRIENDS
An affectionate tribute to the unique and wonderful women we call
"Auntie."
Tamara Traeder and Julienne Bennett
$12.95 ISBN 1-885171-22-6

THE AUNTIES KEEPSAKE BOOK: THE STORY OF OUR FRIENDSHIP
A beautiful way to tell the wonderful story of you and your auntie or
niece.
Tamara Traeder and Julienne Bennett
$19.95 ISBN 1-885171-29-3

LITTLE SISTERS: THE LAST BUT NOT THE LEAST
A feisty look at the trials and tribulations, joys and advantages of

being a little sister.
Carolyn Lieberg
$13.95 ISBN 1-885171-24-2

girlfriends: INVISIBLE BONDS, ENDURING TIES
Filled with true stories of ordinary women and extraordinary friendships, *girlfriends* has become a gift of love among women everywhere.
Carmen Renee Berry and Tamara Traeder
$12.95 ISBN 1-885171-08-0
Also Available: Hardcover gift edition, $20.00 ISBN 1-885171-20-X

girlfriends TALK ABOUT MEN: SHARING SECRETS FOR A GREAT RELATIONSHIP
This book shares insights from real women in real relationships—not just from the "experts."
Carmen Renee Berry and Tamara Traeder
$14.95 ISBN 1-885171-21-8

girlfriends FOR LIFE: FRIENDSHIPS WORTH KEEPING FOREVER
This follow-up to the best-selling *girlfriends* is an all-new collection of stories and anecdotes about the amazing bonds of women's friendships.
Carmen Renee Berry and Tamara Traeder
$13.95 ISBN 1-885171-32-3

A girlfriends GIFT: REFLECTIONS ON THE EXTRAORDINARY BONDS OF FRIENDSHIP
A lively collection of hundreds of quotations from the *girlfriends* books series.
Carmen Renee Berry and Tamara Traeder
$15.95 ISBN 1-885171-43-9

A COUPLE OF FRIENDS: THE REMARKABLE FRIENDSHIP BETWEEN STRAIGHT WOMEN AND GAY MEN
What makes the friendships between straight women and gay men so wonderful? Find out in this honest and fascinating book.
Robert H. Hopcke and Laura Rafaty
$14.95 ISBN 1-885171-33-1

INDEPENDENT WOMEN: CREATING OUR LIVES, LIVING OUR VISIONS
How women value independence and relationship and are redefining
their lives to accommodate both.
Debra Sands Miller
$16.95 ISBN 1-885171-25-0

THOSE WHO CAN...COACH! CELEBRATING COACHES WHO MAKE A
DIFFERENCE
Inspirational stories from men and women who remember a coach
who made a lasting difference in their lives.
Lorraine Glennon and Roy Leavitt
$12.95 ISBN 1-885171-49-8

THOSE WHO CAN...TEACH! CELEBRATING TEACHERS WHO MAKE A
DIFFERENCE
A tribute to our nation's teachers!
Lorraine Glennon and Mary Mohler
$12.95 ISBN 1-885171-35-8

THE WORRYWART'S COMPANION: TWENTY-ONE WAYS TO SOOTHE YOURSELF
AND WORRY SMART
The perfect gift for anyone who lies awake at night worrying.
Dr. Beverly Potter
$11.95 ISBN 1-885171-15-3

DIAMONDS OF THE NIGHT: THE SEARCH FOR SPIRIT IN YOUR DREAMS
Combines the story of "Annie" with a therapist's wisdom about the
power of dreams.
James Hagan, Ph.D.
$16.95 ISBN 1-879290-12-X

Books are available at fine retailers nationwide.

Prices subject to change without notice.